Treasured Inside

Treasured Inside

Copyright © 2024 Denise T. Harper

ISBN 13: 979-8-9898705-0-9

Library of Congress Control Number: 2024900345

Edited by Elizabeth Boerner and Carlene Roche
Cover and layout by Helen Ounjian
Interior author photo by Bill Sammons Jr.
Back cover photo by John Mollura Photography
Additional images by amenic181 from Getty Images for Canva, Amawasri from Getty Images for Canva, and Shen Stock for Canva

All rights reserved. No part of this publication may be reproduced or transmitted in any form or by any means, electronic or mechanical, including photocopy, recording, or any storage and retrieval system now known or to be invented without written permission from the author.

All Scripture quotations, unless otherwise indicated, are taken from the Holy Bible, New International Version®, NIV®. Copyright ©1973, 1978, 1984, 2011 by Biblica, Inc.™ Used by permission of Zondervan. All rights reserved worldwide. www.zondervan.com. The "NIV" and "New International Version" are trademarks registered in the United States Patent and Trademark Office by Biblica, Inc.™

Scripture taken from the Amplified Bible (AMP), Copyright © 2015 by The Lockman Foundation. Used by permission. Scripture quotations marked (CEV) are from the Contemporary English Version Copyright © 1991, 1992, 1995 by American Bible Society, Used by permission. Scripture quotations are from the ESV® Bible (The Holy Bible, English Standard Version®), copyright© 2001 by Crossway Bibles, a publishing ministry of Good News Publishers. Used by permission. All rights reserved. Scripture quotations marked (GNT) are from the Good News Translation in Today's English Version- Second Edition Copyright © 1992 by American Bible Society. Used by permission. Scripture taken from the Holy Bible: International Standard Version©. Copyright © 1996-2012 by The ISV Foundation. ALL RIGHTS RESERVED INTERNATIONALLY. Used by permission. Scripture quotations from The Authorized (King James) Version. Rights in the Authorized Version in the United Kingdom are vested in the Crown. Reproduced by permission of the Crown's patentee, Cambridge University Press. Scripture quotations marked MSG are taken from The Message, copyright © 1993, 2002, 2018 by Eugene H. Peterson. Used by permission of NavPress. All rights reserved. Represented by Tyndale House Publishers. Scripture taken from the New King James Version®. Copyright © 1982 by Thomas Nelson. Used by permission. All rights reserved. Scripture quotations marked (NLT) are taken from the Holy Bible, New Living Translation, copyright © 1996, 2004, 2015 by Tyndale House Foundation. Used by permission of Tyndale House Publishers, Carol Stream, Illinois 60188, USA. All rights reserved. Scripture quotations marked (TLB) are taken from The Living Bible, copyright © 1971 by Tyndale House Foundation. Used by permission of Tyndale House Publishers, Carol Stream, Illinois 60188. All rights reserved. Scripture quotations marked TPT are from The Passion Translation®. Copyright © 2017, 2018, 2020 by Passion & Fire Ministries, Inc. Used by permission. All rights reserved. ThePassionTranslation.com. Scripture taken from The Voice™(VOICE). Copyright © 2012 by Ecclesia Bible Society. Used by permission. All rights reserved.

Perfect Misfits LLC
An Independent Publishing Company
For inquiries, contact perfectmisfits.de@gmail.com

Denise T. Harper

Treasured Inside
Devotions with Denise

This book is dedicated to my husband, Ken, who has kept the drumbeat steady in my life and makes me laugh almost every day.

To my kiddos (who aren't kids any longer) who will always be my favorite people in this world, Cody and Abby. Thank you for being willing to be "show prep" for my radio career and for teaching me so much about what's really important in this life. I adore you both!

To my granddaughter, Macey, who makes my heart skip a little every time we get together.

To my mom and dad, Cathel and Charlie Tanner, who taught me from the day I was born that I am treasured and adored by my Creator, God. You also showed me how to love well… not just by speaking it but also by living it out every day.

To my Father, God, whose Word I cherish and whose presence brings me great peace. Thank You for Your goodness, kindness, and faithfulness in my life. For using the little every day things in my world to show me how often the little things *are* the big things. I treasure You most!

Dear Reader...

It was September 2021, and I had been praying for something new and fresh to share with my friends who listen to the radio station, The Bridge, with whom I have had the privilege of programming and co-hosting weekday mornings for more than a decade at that point. As God is so faithful to do when we ask, He led me to consider what He says about us, as His children. What does God say about you? In less than 30 minutes He had "downloaded" 31 different words or phrases that I knew God's Word had spoken over us. You are loved. You are chosen. You are forgiven. Thirty-one "downloads"! Exactly what I needed to begin the new year with in January 2022.

Once I had the Scripture references I began writing devotional segments that I could share on the air in the mornings, and before I realized what was happening God had ignited a new flame in my heart to use simple, everyday moments to connect the dots to how He reveals Himself to us...every day. Not just the big moments and the difficult moments, but the cleaning out the cupboard, riding to work, and taking a walk with a friend moments too!

God then challenged me to keep on writing. What you are holding in your hands, is the beginning of my response back to Him."Section One" contains those thirty-one reminders of what God says about YOU! It seemed only fitting to begin with what God used to stir up this passion in me.

Thank you for walking this part of the journey with me. We are stronger when we are connected and I am so grateful to have connected with you along the way.

Dedication v
A Letter to My Readers vii

PART ONE
You Are Loved........................3
You Are Enough 6
You Are Forgiven.....................9
You Are Redeemed 10
You Are Rescued.....................11
You Are Beautiful 12
You Are Victorious 14
You Are Strong 16
You Are Amazing 18
You Are Never Alone.................20
You Are Called 23
You Are Treasured...................24
You Are God's Masterpiece 26
You Are Healed.....................28
You Are Handpicked 31
You Are a Citizen of Heaven 32
You Are His........................34
You Are Safe.......................36
You Are Equipped 38
You Are Protected 41
You Are Priceless....................42
You Are Chosen 44
You Are Resilient 46
You Are Known.....................48
You Are Free.......................49
You Are Sealed 50
You Are a New Creation 52
You Are Secure in Christ 54
You Are a Friend of God 56
You Are Comforted 58
You Are Fearless 60

PART TWO

Treasure 64
Authenticity 66
Indelible 68
Broken Crayons. 71
There is a Cost 72
I Can't Wait for You to Read This 76
Coffee Dates & Losing Weight 78
In the Quiet 80
Gracelaced. 82
I Can Do It!. 84
Two Bananas and a Smile 86
Come and See. 90
Where You Sit. 93
Inspector 25 94
All In!. 95
Stay Where I Can See You 96
Airplane Mode 99
Just Stay Calm. 100
Collecting What's Important. 102
Unlikely Company. 104
The Unforced Rhythms of Grace 106
The Old Orange Jar 108
YOU ARE SPEEDING! 110
Generous Giving, Generous Living. 112
What's In a Nap?. 114
In the Waiting 116
Casting 118
Having a Spotter 120
Lessons from a Toddler 122
Under Pressure 124
Tyranny of the Urgent 126

PART THREE
Refreshment 130
Put Your Oxygen Mask on First 132
The Gift of Rest. 134
The One Whom Jesus Loved 136
Just a Little T-L-C. 138
Sneak Attacks 140
Safe Harbor. 142
Judging Covers 144
What Kind of Morning Is It? 146
Guilt-Free Timekeeping 148
Live In the Flow. 150
Giving Up Your Seat 152
Surprise and Delight 154
Dream Home 156
The Race. 158
What Is Your Ministry?. 160
Unfinished 162
The Hard Word. 164
The Scent of Stress 166
Holding Patterns 168
Early Bird Specials. 171
Lingering Longer 172
Clear Plastic Covers. 174
One Lost Sheep. 176
When Good Isn't Good Enough 178
Parking in A7 180
Lessons from the Fishbowl 182
Junk Drawers. 184
Sticky Notes 186
My Japanese Maple 188

BONUS SECTION: A Place Set Just for You
Falling in Love. 192
Practice Makes Perfect. 194
A Mile in Your Shoes. 196
I Could Never Handle That 198
Traditions 200
Repurposed. 202
Truth Is Quiet 205

About Denise T. Harper. 208

Part One

You Are Loved

My earliest memory of feeling loved was when I was three years old. I know I was 3 because my brother was just a baby and we were coming home from my grandmother's family Christmas Eve dinner. It was a treasured tradition in our family to gather at her home for dinner and gift-giving. That year it snowed so hard that on our way home that night we got stuck in it. Once stuck, we were within walking distance from home, so Mom and Dad decided to leave the car and walk. What they couldn't see was some sort of pole or tree across the road buried beneath the snow. DOWN they went... and because they were carrying us, so did WE!

What I remember about that night was being *really, really* cold. Dad started a fire in the fireplace and then let me curl up in his lap by the fire. Mom brought out hot chocolate to help warm us up. Safe. Warm. Loved. That's the first time I remember feeling comforted and at 3 years old... that felt like the best kind of love.

Life is full of unexpected circumstances. We can be caught off guard, even stumble and take a spill because of unseen obstacles in our path. But we can be sure that our Heavenly Father never lets go of us. We are never separated from His care.

His promise is that we are loved:

> *I'm absolutely convinced that nothing- nothing living or dead, angelic or demonic, today or tomorrow, high or low, thinkable or unthinkable- absolutely nothing can get between us and God's love because of the way that Jesus our Master has embraced us.*
>
> Romans 8:38 MSG

What does God say about you?...You are loved.

nothing can get between us and God's love

You Are Enough

Isn't it crazy that we can receive a dozen compliments and yet a single negative or critical comment can totally derail us?! Sometimes it's not anyone else's voice that causes us to shut down. It's our *own* voice that leaves us diminished and feeling inadequate.

We need to remind ourselves that we are made in the image of God. (Genesis 1:27) That's right. You and I bear the image of God within us! The enemy of our soul wants to discredit God's work in us. Don't let him do it! To everything God created He saw that it is good. When He formed and breathed life into Adam. God saw it was very good.

What we see as weakness in ourselves, God sees as strength. That's the very point that we must lean in to receive His strength and because of Him, we ARE enough. The very places in us that are lacking are exactly where the power of Christ can shine brightest.

> *Each time He said, "I am with you; that is all you need. My power shows up best in weak people." Now I am glad to boast about how weak I am; I am glad to be a living demonstration of Christ's power, instead of showing off my own power and abilities.*
>
> 2 Corinthians 12:9 TLB

What does God say about you?... You are enough.

Jesus made a way

You Are Forgiven

Growing up on the east coast it was always easy for me to get my bearings. The ocean and the spectacular sunrise served as a type of compass for me. Later, when my husband, Ken, and I went on a Caribbean cruise we spent several days at sea between ports. I'll never forget walking the deck of this enormous ship. No matter which direction I looked, or how hard my eyes strained to see land off in the distance, there was no land in sight. What direction were we heading? In the middle of the day when the sun was directly overhead it was impossible to know without an actual compass.

The one thing that struck me that first day was that there was no dividing line from east to west. I could turn around 360 degrees and only see the ocean. There was no way to tell where the east ended and the west began! I was reminded of that promise in Psalm 103:12, *As far as the east is from the west, so far has He removed our transgressions from us.* There is no dividing line between what kind of sin or how often we've sinned. The truth is that we were born sinners… in desperate need of a Savior. His name is Jesus; and because He lived a sinless life, died on the cross for every one of us - taking on our sins, and then rose again, we can be saved. Jesus made a way for our relationship with God to be restored. The only way for imperfect us to be reconnected with the one true and perfect God is through Jesus and because of Him, we are saved.

What does God say about you? When you receive Christ as your Savior… you are forgiven.

You Are Redeemed

I am the queen of saving coupons and gift cards. I like to tuck them away for a "special" occasion. I can't begin to tell you how many coupons expired and businesses closed without me ever using them for the savings they were meant to bring me. There's no one to blame but myself. I fully had the capability to enjoy the benefits of those gift cards and coupons. I chose not to use them. Maybe not intentionally, but putting off using them is still the same.

Romans 3:24 tells us *ALL are justified freely by His grace through the redemption that came by Christ Jesus.* ALL means every one of us and justified freely means... well, it means that the cost of our freedom was paid for, and our redemption from the bondage of sin is available to us through Christ. But there is a choice to be made, and no one can make it for us. We have to *choose* to receive that redemption. We can hear about it, learn about it, and consider receiving it on some other day, but unless we choose to accept His grace, freely given for our redemption, we *choose* to stand unjustified, separate from God. When you choose Him, you are taking full advantage of the gift that Christ Jesus paid for with His life.

What does God say about you? In Him...You are redeemed.

You Are Rescued

When we are young, we hear stories about princesses and the warriors who save them. Little girls want to be the princess whom the warrior defends. Little boys want to be the warrior who slays the dragon. Then we grow up. It becomes harder and harder to believe we are a princess worthy of defending or a warrior courageous enough to win the fight.

But you and I...we are royalty. We are the King's kids. Yes, the world can be frightening and cruel. Yes, there will be hard days... that may turn into hard months... and even harder years. Some days will feel like a dream. Other days will seem to never end. But there is One who never leaves our side. He is our Victor. His name is Jesus. He is strong and mighty to save us. Whether we are a princess or a warrior, or maybe a warrior princess, we all need our Warrior Jesus to save us. And indeed He did!!

He has rescued us from the dominion of darkness and brought us into the kingdom of the Son He loves (Colossians 1:13).

What does God say about you? ...You are rescued.

You Are Beautiful

Little white lights strung over a patio in the backyard, a sunrise over the ocean, an orchestra playing your favorite song. Watching the sunset regardless of how good or how hard the day has been. For the moments that we pause to take in that miracle of extraordinary closure of the experiences and emotions of another number on the calendar… for that brief space, we forget about the day and are held captive by the beauty of the moment.

It is rare that we describe someone as "beautiful." Babies are beautiful. Brides are beautiful. A married couple renewing their vows after being together for decades… that is beautiful. All of these are moments in time. We often tend to judge "beauty" by those rare exceptional moments; but rarely do we acknowledge and take time to appreciate the beauty in the ordinary, everyday lives around us.

WE are His most valuable art. So precious are we to Him that He chose to send His only Son, Jesus, to die in our place so we can live forever with Him. His Spirit, inside of us, makes us uniquely beautiful. Not beauty that is skin deep... but beauty that radiates from way down deep in our soul. Ecclesiastes 3:11 (ESV) tells us that *He [God] has made everything beautiful in its time.*

What does God say about you?... You are beautiful.

You Are Victorious

The dictionary defines victorious as triumphant. I envision a massive wave of cheering… an energetic celebration following a BIG win. THAT'S a LOT of energy. Is it even possible to keep that level of triumph up day after day?

When I was looking up the word "victorious," I read the FAQ below the definition, "You use the word victorious to describe someone who has won a victory in a struggle, war or competition." Well, my goodness, wouldn't you agree that, *every day* you and I are faced with at least one struggle? Some days we are definitely feeling as though we are at war with our spouse, our kids, our parents… ourselves! And should we even bring up the competition factor?! If we're not competing with our co-workers or our neighbors, we are absolutely competing for the fast lane on the highway or the parking space up front!

EVERY DAY... there is a struggle... a battle for our hearts, our minds, and our souls. But listen to what 1 Corinthians 15:57 declares over you and me, *Thanks be to God! He gives us the victory through our Lord Jesus Christ.* Because He is the same yesterday, today, and forever... I believe that promise is for today, and tomorrow, and the next day... and God *GIVES US* the victory! Don't miss those two words in His promise. We can get up this morning and thank God for the victory. Expect the victory. Watch for it! And when we receive it through Christ... we celebrate and thank Him again! Because Jesus triumphed... so can we!

What does God say about you?... You are victorious.

You Are Strong

When I was a kid one of my favorite Saturday morning cartoons was Popeye the Sailor Man. Do you remember what made him strong? Of course, it was the spinach! That cartoon had to have been crafted by a mom trying to find a clever way to get her kids to like spinach… and *eat it!*

How about the Bible character Samson? Remember the link to his strength? We might shorten the story by saying he was strong because he never cut his hair. But his strength wasn't really in his long locks. His strength resulted from God's blessing on him as he took his vows to follow God seriously with an outward sign of never cutting his hair. You can read the story of Samson in Judges 13.

We might consider a strong person one who can lift a lot of weights in the gym or one who can hike up a massive mountain. But strength is not only measured by our physical muscle capabilities. Some of the strongest people I've known in my life are not mountain climbers, weightlifters, or even daily workout champions. The true strength of a person can also be measured by what is on the *inside*. The one who can withstand the many attacks of an often unpredictable, ever-ruthless enemy. The one who has the strength to stand when the cacophony of voices keeps saying, "You are not good enough, rich enough, pretty enough, smart enough." But, hear this truth from our Father in Philippians 4:13, *I can do all things through Him who strengthens me.* ALL THINGS. You and I can face enormous attacks and subtle attacks because we will never face them alone. Because Jesus Christ is the One inside of us who makes us able to walk through every situation that seems bigger than us. Because HE is bigger than every situation.

What does God say about you?... You are strong.

You Are Amazing

One of my favorite words in the English language is the word "amazing." It almost demands an exclamation point at the end. It makes me think that whatever we are attaching that description to is well beyond what we thought it could be. For instance, our vacation was *amazing!* The band put on an *amazing* show! This new coffee flavor is *amazing!*

How about the amazing grace of God? His grace is far beyond what we could ever think or imagine. Once we've encountered His *amazing grace...* our lives are never the same. The grace of God is so incredibly complex and yet so very simple. We could speak a lifetime and not explain the complexity of His grace, yet when the Master of the Universe whispers to our heart, His divine invitation to receive His grace in exchange for all of our sins, all we need to say is simply, "Yes."

As His creation, you and I are made in His image. Psalm 139:4 (TPT) says,

> *I thank You, God, for making me so mysteriously complex! Everything You do is marvelously breathtaking. It simply amazes me to think about it! How thoroughly You know me, Lord!*

There is that description again of being more than what we ever thought we could be... mysteriously complex... and yet so simple.

What does God say about you?... You are amazing!

You Are Never Alone

Have you ever thought about what David meant when he wrote in Psalm 23: *Though I walk through the valley of the shadow of death...?* Sounds ominous, doesn't it? I hadn't felt the full weight of that space until recently. My sister-in-law and I kept vigil for nearly 48 hours, while my youngest brother lay dying in a hospital bed. We sat beside him, praying, reminiscing, hoping for a miracle, weeping, laughing, reading scripture, and playing worship music. Everything we tried to do to bring him, and each other, comfort. We walked with him as far as we could in this life. I knew the moment he took his last breath, and his first forever step into eternity, that he was embraced fully by the arms of His Savior.

Never alone. Sometimes God allows us to keep each other company but even when there is no one around... we are *never* alone. Jesus said this in Matthew 28:20 (NLT), *"Be sure of this: I am with you always, even to the end of the age."* He never leaves us!

Even when I thought I couldn't endure that valley as the death shadow passed over me… I knew God's presence was there. He was holding me close… close enough that I could feel His heartbeat. I've never felt the veil between this life and the heavenly realm feel as thin as it did that day and in those days following such loss. In Psalm 34:18 God said, *He is near the brokenhearted and He saves the crushed in spirit.*

Loss can come from so many things. You may have suffered the loss of a loved one, perhaps a job loss, the letting go of a dream, a marriage, or a home. In all of it, God is with us. He is not limited by time or space as we are. He is Emmanuel, God with us.

What does God say about you?… You are never alone.

Our calling is who we are!

You Are Called

What is a "calling"? Often when we find ourselves doing something we really enjoy that makes a difference in the lives of the people around us we might say that we have "found our calling," our "destiny." Discovering our purpose in life becomes the grand pursuit of growing up. What do *you* want to be when you grow up?

This is not to be confused with the profession we train, study, and work to pursue. That's what we DO. *Our calling is who we are!* We are called by God.

Romans 8:28 reads, *And we know that in all things God works for the good of those who love Him, who have been called according to His purpose.* That is usually the version that I quote as I focus on the promise that God is working everything out for our good and His glory.

When I was a kid I memorized *The King James Version* of Romans 8:28. It goes like this: *And we know that all things work together for good to them that love God, to them who are the called according to His purpose.* I never quite understood that phrase when I was younger... "to them who are THE CALLED." But now that I do, I LOVE that! That is you and me! We are called by God... to God. It is not something we do or something we work to achieve. We are His.

What does God say about you?... You are called.

You Are Treasured

Without me knowing it, my husband Ken, had gotten an old, worn travel trunk from my parent's basement, that once belonged to my great-grandmother, and had it restored to give to me for Christmas one year. The one who restored it also included before and after photos along with a history of the type of trunk it was; a ladies' trunk, because it had compartments inside that were for a parasol, a hat, and undergarments. Because of the embossed tin on the exterior, it is thought to have been used as far back as the late 1800s.

Seeing it on Christmas morning brought me to tears. I loved that Ken had pulled off such a wonderfully thoughtful surprise gift *and* that I had a beautifully restored family heirloom to cherish. I have treasured that trunk over the years. Not only have I always given it a place of prominence in my home but I have used it to store cherished keepsakes inside as well.

For you are a people holy to the Lord your God. Out of all the peoples on the face of the earth, the Lord has chosen you to be His treasured possession.

Deuteronomy 14:2

    He has chosen you and me. Weary travelers. Worn from the journey and maybe even considered worthless by some of the world's standards; but not by God's. We are His. He chose you and me to be His own. So valuable to Him that He sent His only Son, Jesus, to live and die and be raised again to life, so that we could be restored in our relationship with Him. That's the best restoration story ever!

    What does God say about you?… You are treasured.

You Are God's Masterpiece

Whenever I hear the word "masterpiece" I still think of the sweet, tender song that Christian artist Sandi Patti recorded in 1989, for her firstborn child, Ana. It may have even been sung over you at your baby dedication if you were born in the '90s. My favorite lyric in the song: "He breathed in you a song and to make it all complete, He brought the masterpiece into the world. You are a masterpiece, a new creation He has formed."

It is written in Ephesians 2:10 (NLT), *For we are God's masterpiece. He has created us anew in Christ Jesus, so we can do the good things He planned for us long ago.* There are so many wonderful things packed into that little verse. You were never unplanned. God not only *planned* your creation, He formed every single part of you. He also planned so many good things for you to accomplish long before anyone even knew you were a possibility! You have a Kingdom purpose! And, accepting His Son, Christ Jesus, as your Savior makes you a new creation.

We could use that Bible verse in our prayer today: "Thank You, God, that I am Your masterpiece. That You created me and You have a master plan for my life. Don't let me miss a single thing that You have planned for me to do! And all the glory goes to You, Lord. Amen."

What does God say about you?... You are God's Masterpiece.

"He breathed in you a song"

You Are Healed

I had a Sunday School teacher who used to say, "Instead of saying, 'I think I'm catching a cold!' start saying, 'I think I'm catching a *healing*!'" It IS a mindset, you know. We could go either way in our beliefs. Is it because we condition ourselves to expect the worst? Maybe hoping to avoid discouragement perhaps?

The truth is Christ finished the work of our healing on the cross. In 1 Peter 2:24 it is written, *He himself bore our sins in His body on the cross, so that we might die to sins and live for righteousness; by His wounds you have been healed.* Some Bible translations read, "You *were* healed." Our greatest healing need is for our soul. Christ's death and resurrection made that possible if we will only acknowledge and receive it.

Every other healing that we would need in this life was purchased by His stripes (wounds). The prophet Isaiah, told us in the Old Testament, *by His wounds we are healed.* (Isaiah 53:5) Notice Peter quotes Isaiah but makes one change in the statement. He said, "By His wounds, we have been healed." Our healing has already happened… we're just not yet walking fully in it!

Sometimes our healing is delayed. We don't always understand His ways. If there is a delay we can be sure it is not without purpose. God never wastes a moment of our pain or suffering. He will redeem it. Ultimately, you and I will be completely healed… made whole… because of what Jesus did for us on the cross. Healing may come for us today, in an instant, or most certainly when we receive our ultimate healing from this life to eternity.

What does God say about you?… You are healed.

I chose you and appointed you

You Are Handpicked

I love picking out fruits and vegetables in the grocery store. I avoid the bags and containers of produce. Because, you know that while some of them may be just right, there will undoubtedly be a few rotten ones in the bunch. Hand-selecting produce ensures that we should get the very best of the best. So we pick them up for inspection. Do they look good? Do they feel right? No bruises. No soft spots. We might take "seconds" in canned goods but seconds in fresh produce is just not acceptable.

Get this! The Bible says that we are handpicked… by the Master Gardener, Himself! John 15:6 says:

> *"You did not choose Me, but I chose you and appointed you so that you might go and bear fruit - fruit that will last - and so that whatever you ask in My name the Father will give you."*

What a promise! We are chosen by God to bear fruit, not fruit that goes rotten but fruit that will last. Chosen, appointed by God, fruit-bearers. That's an amazing thought! The next time you are feeling overlooked or unseen. Remember what John 15:6 tells us.

What does God say about you?… You are handpicked.

You Are a Citizen of Heaven

My first passport arrived and I was so excited! Other than the inside front page, which had my photo ID along with who I was and my citizenship details, the book was empty. But as I leafed through the book, blank page after blank page, I could just envision the possibilities. All of the countries I could visit and the endless stories I would tell!

As I have traveled to different countries, each country has turned a page and, with its own unique stamp, stamped my passport giving me permission to access its border, connect with its people and experience its own unique flavor and character. The customs stamp declares to anyone who asks that I am approved to *visit* but my cover page shouts in bold print that I *do not belong* there.

While I have enjoyed my visits to other countries there is nothing like coming home. There is nothing like handing my passport to an officer at customs when entering my home country and proudly showing that I am a citizen of the United States of America. I belong here.

But even "here" is temporary. As a believer, this world is just a temporary stay. We have access to its sights, its people, and experiences day after day, after month, after year. But our real home is Heaven. Philippians 3:20 is clear, *But our citizenship is in Heaven. And we eagerly await a Savior from there, the Lord Jesus Christ.* Our passport may be filled with colorful experiences and connections from all of our travels here in this life, but if you could see the seal of the Holy Spirit on our hearts it would *clearly* spell out where we truly belong.

What does God say about you?... You are a citizen of Heaven.

You Are His

There's nothing wrong with being independent. We should know how to take care of ourselves. It's what our parents teach us and what we, in turn, teach our children. But there is something in our spiritual DNA that leaves us searching, if we don't find the connection we were created to make and preserve with our Creator.

In our search to connect, we might make choices that lead us in the wrong direction, but if we will choose to seek God we will find Him. He longs for us to seek Him with all of our heart. One of my favorite verses in the Bible is an amazing word picture. Imagine this verse from Genesis 3:8 (NLT) about Adam and Eve in the garden, *When the cool evening breezes were blowing, the man and his wife heard the Lord God walking about in the garden.* Of course, that was right after they had disobeyed God's instruction, and everything for them, as well as for all of humanity, was about to change forever. But imagine that was a daily routine that they would connect with God… *every day,* in the cool evening breezes, maybe with a glass of sweet tea on their front porch.

Things changed that day and the entire Bible is filled with the stories of men and women on their search back to find connection with their Creator. When Jesus came to earth, He restored our relationship with God. We can walk with God in the cool of the evening, as the sun is rising, while we're driving to work, over our lunch break, or wherever we are willing to make a space for Him. God is with us, always.

Through Christ, God redeemed us, each one, and we don't need to live in fear of anything. Jesus restored our connection with God! Isaiah 43:1 tells us God's Word through the prophet Isaiah: *Do not fear, for I have redeemed you; I have called you by name; you are mine.*

What does God say about you?… You are His.

You Are Safe

What does "safe" mean to you? The more I've thought about what it means to feel "safe," I realize that there is an action that must occur first; we must trust. Trust in something or someone must occur for us to feel safe.

How do we know that we can eat or drink the foods and beverages we have in our pantry and refrigerator without getting sick? We read the label and have a level of trust that the contents inside are exactly what the label tells us. We read the safety features on a new vehicle, a bicycle, or a stroller for our newborn… and we trust that the manufacturer has presented all the safety features and cautions that we need to consider before purchasing.

How do we know that we are safe in God's care? We read His Word. It's got all the ingredients of our life listed, along with all the many safety features, and comes loaded with cautions to direct us and help keep us safe on our journey. The question is what level of trust do we put in our Savior? His promises are *trust*worthy and we can be sure that if God said it… we can believe it! We can trust Him.

There are so many promises in God's Word about being safe in Him. Proverbs 18:10 (NKJV), is one of my favorites: *The name of the Lord is a strong tower. The righteous run into it and are safe.*

What does God say about you?… You are safe!

You Are Equipped

I have had this recurring dream over the years. I walk out onto an empty stage with a spotlight on me and a room full of people and I can't remember *anything* that I'm supposed to say. Not...one...word. Talk about stage fright! The first time I remember it happening I was preparing for a fifteen-minute monologue that I was going to be acting out on stage at a dinner theatre. It was so far out of my comfort zone that no matter how much I prepared for that moment I continued to battle the fear that I would walk out on that stage and forget every word of it!

Even though I spent hours memorizing and preparing for that presentation I still remember the nightmare and that fear of being unprepared. The fear was real to me but the reality was I had invested the time and I was prepared for that moment. I had to choose faith over fear to accomplish the task I was called to do.

So it is in living our lives for God. Each of us is called by God to do good things to fulfill His plan for us. How do we prepare? How can we be ready when an opportunity presents itself? And make no mistake. There will be many opportunities every day to do good things! Spend time soaking up God's Word! 2 Timothy 3:16-17 tells us the answer:

> *All Scripture is God-breathed and is useful for teaching, rebuking, correcting and training in righteousness, so that the servant of God may be thoroughly equipped for every good work.*

No matter what your stage looks like… a kitchen, a classroom, an office, a construction site, or a boardroom… you are not alone. If you'll take the time to hear what God wants to say to you through His Word, you will find that you are more prepared than you ever thought possible. Choose faith over fear today.

What does God say about you?… You are equipped.

God gives us a place

You Are Protected

When I was a kid I remember walking in a crowded parking lot of the shopping center with my mom. She would want me to walk closest to the parked cars in the lot. She would position herself between me and any vehicles driving through the lane as we were walking. When I became a parent and my kids got old enough to walk alongside me, whether it was a parking lot, or on a sidewalk, it was just a natural thing for me to put myself between my child and any oncoming traffic. You've probably done the same.

So it is with our Heavenly Father. God gives us a place to know we are safe when there is danger present. He goes even further in helping us to know His comfort. See if you can just envision what Psalm 32:7 reveals to us: *You are my hiding place; You will protect me from trouble and surround me with songs of deliverance.* What a beautiful picture of His peace surrounding us when there is trouble nearby. He surrounds us with songs of deliverance! How many times have you and I heard the right song at just the right time? What if that is the Lord singing a song of deliverance over you at just the moment you need it most?

What does God say about you?… You are protected.

You Are Priceless

Have you ever heard someone say, "God knows the number of hairs on your head"? If you're fairly new in your relationship with the Lord you might not have heard that yet. But I can remember when I was a kid thinking that was an odd thing to say. Like who really cares how many hairs are on my head?! Well, as I've gotten older I realize that the number of hairs on our head can change rather rapidly on any given day. It's just one of *many* things we might find concerning us from day to day.

Luke 12:6-7 reads:

> *Five sparrows are sold for just two pennies, but God doesn't forget even one of them. Even the hairs on your head are counted. So don't be afraid! You are worth much more than many sparrows.*

In the time that the Gospel of Luke was written when someone purchased five sparrows that fifth little bird was free because one sparrow alone had no value. But even that single sparrow that we might say had no value, was valuable to God. He watches over and cares for every little thing... and that includes everything about you and me as well.

If God cares about the little things, imagine how He responds to the big things. We can be sure that God is keeping track of all of it. For even the hairs on our heads are counted. So don't be afraid! That's what He said. Do - not - fear! For you are worth *much more* than many sparrows.

What does God say about you?... You are priceless.

You Are Chosen

Auditioning for a part in the choir or a role in the play. Are you having flashbacks yet? How about gym class in fourth grade when you were selected halfway through... or maybe left till last? Whether you are being interviewed for a job or hoping to just not be the last one left to be added to the team in gym class... there is a common thread that tries to weave its way through our minds. The needle of rejection can pierce our spirit, even from the time of our youth, with a thread that sews words on our hearts like unwanted, unacceptable, untalented, or unskilled.

The stress and strain of rejection, even the possibility of it, leaves a mark. Each time it marks us, the patch labeled "not enough" grows deeper and wider over our hearts and in our minds. Until one day that wound of rejection holds more power over us than the inspiration of any dream we ever dared believe could come true. It can hold us hostage from becoming who God fully intended us to become.

There is ONE truth that trumps every rejection, cancels every negative word, heals every wound we've experienced in this life… and can set us free if we will allow it! The truth: we are loved by God and He has chosen us! 1 Thessalonians 1:4 says, *For we know, brothers and sisters, loved by God, that He has chosen you.* God has a plan for your life and He has chosen you! And consider this, some of the rejection we've experienced may be because we've set our sights too low! Maybe God is paving the way for His higher and better plans! After all, you are the ONLY one God chose to live the life that only YOU can live.

What does God say about you?… You are chosen.

You Are Resilient

I started reading an article about the strategies of being resilient. The word "strategies" made me expect monumental steps to achieve resiliency. To my surprise, I saw things like "be mindful to breathe, to eat, to move... to practice one small step at a time." My first reaction was, "Well, duh!" But as I thought about it more I found myself agreeing that being resilient isn't achieved by giant leaps and bounds. Resilience is the steadiness of keeping on.

The Bible uses the word picture of a tree:

> "Blessed is the man who trusts in the Lord, whose trust is the Lord. He is like a tree planted by water, that sends out its roots by the stream, and does not fear when heat comes, for its leaves remain green, and is not anxious in the year of drought, for it does not cease to bear fruit."
>
> Jeremiah 17:7-8 ESV

Regardless of the heat or drought, even when it was only a seed covered up by dirt, surrounded in darkness, it kept growing, focusing on being planted, not buried, digging roots deep toward the river, to withstand heat and drought, fear and anxiety. *And* it does not cease to bear fruit. When you hear that verse do you imagine a Charlie Brown tree or a healthy, vibrant, growing tree that is rich in fruit? Perhaps we need to adjust how we see ourselves if we are putting our trust in the Lord each day. If we are, we are much more like that tree described in Jeremiah 17:7-8. You know, the one that keeps on keeping on, despite the situations surrounding it, digging deep... bearing fruit.

What does God say about you?... You are resilient.

You Are Known

The first time my husband, Ken, and I heard our baby's heartbeat, our hearts flooded with so much joy. We didn't know if it was a boy or a girl. In fact, we didn't really know anything about this little gift except that he or she was filled with possibilities and promise. When we brought home the first sonogram picture, in small print along the edge, the typed words "Baby Harper" were written. Once he was born, the nurse placed him in a hospital bassinet with a blue cap on his head and a note card that read "Baby Boy Harper."

Once that name card was replaced with one that declared he would be known from that day forward as Cody Thomas Harper it launched his pursuit to be known not just by his name but for who he is and his contributions to the world.

We are each born with a desire to be known and a need to be loved. When we are born not even our mama or our daddy knows who we are or what we will become. But there is One who has known us since before the beginning of time. Jeremiah 1:5 says, *Before I formed you in the womb I knew you, before you were born I set you apart*. So today focus on the fact that God created you and knows you. Indeed He set you apart for a specific and vital purpose.

What does God say about you?... You are known.

You Are Free

There is so much in this life that can imprison us. We are not just bound by physical confines. Many of us are held captive by fear, by our past, by our sins. Even our accomplishments can hold us back from walking into what the future holds for us. It's true. We can spend so much time living in the past that we become unable to live in the present and unwilling to embrace the future.

Even the most generous, loving, gracious people on earth are prisoners to sin. The Bible sets the boundaries that we are ALL sinners in need of a Savior. Jesus knew that without His sacrifice on the cross, we would never be able to pay the debt to set ourselves free. And that is why He came… to pay the debt that only He could pay to set us free forever. John 8:36 is a precious promise for you and me that is the key to unlock the door forever! *So if the Son sets you free, you will be free indeed.*

What does God say about you?… You are free.

You Are Sealed

We can definitely be swayed by a seal. Let's talk bananas for a minute. You could see a bunch of bananas that look pretty good. You start to reach for them... and then you see the bunch marked with a Chiquita Banana seal. Let's face it. You don't know anything about that first bunch... but the Chiquita seal gives you confidence for what awaits you inside its bananas.

The Cambridge Dictionary defines a seal as, "A mark or symbol on a product showing that it has been tested by an official (organization), and has been found to be of the right standard." An official performed a thorough inspection and determined it to meet its standard. Then placed its seal on it as a sign to everyone that it has been selected to carry its name and all that it represents.

When we receive Christ as our Savior, our Father God, who already knows us inside and out, sees Christ in us, and sets His seal of the Holy Spirit on us. We bear His name, Christian. His Spirit, revealed through us, is a sign to everyone we meet that we belong to Him.

Ephesians 1:13 tells us that it is so:

> *And you also were included in Christ when you heard the message of truth, the gospel of your salvation. When you believed, you were marked in Him with a seal, the promised Holy Spirit.*

What does God say about you?... You are sealed.

You Are a New Creation

From the time we can stand up in our mama's high heels, dress up in something sparkly, and sneak into her makeup kit to add the boldest, brightest lipstick to our smile it becomes a fascination… this idea of playing dress-up. Makeovers. Modeling and re-modeling.

As grown-ups, we may still love to dress up for special occasions but to keep up that appearance day in and day out?… Well, it's just too hard. TOO much work! We tend to be most comfortable in the "what you see is what you get," one-size-fits-most look. We can experience the most luxurious spa day with ALL the add-on treatments included, or change our hair color; we can even wear contact lenses that change our eye color. But at the end of the day, all of that is only skin deep. None of that really changes who we are.

One encounter with Jesus Christ and we are changed *completely*, from the inside out, forever! We learn in 2 Corinthians 5:17 (ESV), *Therefore, if anyone is in Christ, he is a new creation. The old has passed away; behold, the new has come.* A heart changed by Jesus *beats* differently. The old heart that kept time only for what it wanted for itself is gone. The new heart beats in a rhythm that syncs with its Savior's heart. To love more like Him. We are changed from the inside out. And that beauty changes us forever!

What does God say about you?… You are a new creation.

You Are Secure in Christ

I grew up in the era of "Layaway Plans." Mom picked out the item or items she wanted, like Christmas presents, or big-ticket items like a new stereo system. The store would keep her items and, over time, she made payments on them until the balance was paid off and then she got to bring her items home. She didn't get the goods until she paid in full.

The first time I bought a car, a MAJOR big ticket item, I was introduced to the "installment" plan. I made a down payment, and I drove the car off the lot THAT DAY after agreeing that I would continue to pay installments until the car was completely paid off. The down payment was a show of good faith that I would make good on my guarantee to pay the full balance due. And I got to drive it right away!

As believers, we have entered into an installment plan, of sorts, with God. Think about this: The promise of eternity is ours when we choose Christ as our Savior. We may not walk "into" eternity for years but God's promises are ours to receive the more we grow in Him. 2 Corinthians 1:22 from the New Living Translation tells us, *He has identified us as His own by placing the Holy Spirit in our hearts as the first installment that guarantees everything He has promised us.*

Don't you love that? As His, He places His Spirit in our hearts, as a good faith first installment guaranteeing everything He promised us. That is huge! And we get to live it every day between now and eternity!

What does God say about you?... You are secure in Christ.

You Are a Friend of God

We were trying out a brand new restaurant and we scored BIG. It was fabulous, with ambiance, amazing food, and great service. Oliver was our server and he was always there when we needed something. We enjoyed a nice, light conversation with him whenever he was nearby. The conversation my friend and I were having over our meal was personal so anytime that Oliver stopped by to check on us we switched gears to chat with him. Oliver was our server, doing a great job, and he was friendly. But he wasn't our friend.

Being friendly doesn't make you a friend. It might be a first step toward friendship but real friendship is cultivated over time through experiences and by building trust.

I love envisioning Jesus around a table with His disciples who had spent three years following Him everywhere He went, helping Him, serving Him, and learning how to be a God follower. Jesus knew His death was imminent and these final conversations with His closest companions were so important to convey His heart for them.

In John 15:15, Jesus wanted them to open their hearts to more and to realize the depth of His love for them. He said,

> *"I no longer call you servants because a servant does not know his master's business. Instead, I have called you friends, for everything that I learned from my Father I have made known to you."*

That word is for us today as well. We serve God out of love and a desire to obey… but don't forget that He has called us His *friend*. Make time to sit with Him today and listen for His Word to speak to you.

What does God say about you?… You are a friend of God.

You Are Comforted

The word comfort is used in a number of ways. Are you comfortable? What is your comfort level with this? I've resorted to comfort foods. This has all the creature comforts you could want! I found such comfort in it. See what I mean? Comfort could refer to anything from macaroni & cheese to a sleep number bed to stress-free or chill time with your favorite person.

When someone suffers loss we pray that God will bring them peace… and comfort. But what exactly does that mean? What does God's comfort look like? What does it feel like? I think that when God comforts us it can look and feel different to every person in every situation. We all have our own way we need to be comforted. And God knows what we need and exactly when we need it.

God's comfort may come in the form of a call from a dear friend, or finding a letter, a poem, or a journal left behind by someone that we love and miss. His comfort could be through a song or a scripture that He leads us to or reminds us of at just-the-moment we need it. There are countless numbers of ways that God reaches from the heavens to fill the void beside us, and inside us, when we need comfort. And no one knows what we need better than the One who created us.

If we are willing, God will even allow us to be a part of His comforting process with others. When we realize that He has entrusted us with the ability to comfort another, what a beautiful blessing it is to get a glimpse of the reason why we encountered the pain and endured the healing process… to help comfort someone else.

2 Corinthians 1:3-4 promises:

> *The God of all comfort, comforts us in all our troubles, so that we can comfort those in any trouble with the comfort we ourselves receive from God.*

What does God say about you?… You are comforted.

You Are Fearless

What makes you afraid? Things I fear include snakes, tight spaces, and revolving doors. I can trace back to when the fear of snakes first occurred but I don't have a specific event I can point to about the other two. Other than that, I dread both and would do just about anything to avoid either.

Some fears could be in place to help us stay safe. We might call them healthy fears… maybe more like common sense. But many fears are unhealthy and can keep us from experiencing some of the most amazing things that God wants for us to live out. So how do we overcome fear?

The one thing that blots out fear is FAITH. The only way to set that in motion is to choose it! Sounds easy at first: Faith over fear. But unfortunately choosing faith over fear isn't a "one and done" decision. We have to resolve to choose faith again and again… and again; in the little things and the big things.

We must choose to have faith that God is who He says He is and that His love for us is higher and better, richer and more enduring than anything else in this world. We must choose our faith in God over what we fear now, an hour from now, tomorrow, next month, or next year. In this life, there will always be things we must face, and choose faith over fear.

Psalm 27:1 (CEV) is a promise we can lean into no matter what our fear tells us: *You, Lord, are the light that keeps me safe. I am not afraid of anyone. You protect me, and I have no fears.* God is our light and our protector. With Him, we can declare that we have NO fears.

What does God say about you?... You are fearless.

Faith over fear

Part Two

Treasure

Almost every day I drive through this same intersection. But on one particular day, while I was waiting for the light to change, I glanced at a thrift shop on the corner. Nothing unusual. I've passed by it hundreds of times. Every day someone carries out used furniture, gadgets, wheel covers, and a variety of things hoping to catch my attention and entice me to stop and look. What caught my eye as I waited for the light to change was a piece of white picket fence propped up at the corner of the lot, an old weathered flower garland woven thru the wooden slats, with an equally weather-beaten sign that read, "Thrift Store - Open Daily - Treasures Inside." From the outside a hodgepodge of what some might consider junk. Things the original owner no longer considered of value. But my curiosity was peaked! What *was* inside? Could it be something I'd always hoped I'd find? Treasure?

Treasure can be a thing. A quantity of precious metals, gems, or other valuables according to Webster's Dictionary. But it's also an action: to keep carefully, to cherish or hold dear. To value greatly (also Webster). The remainder of my drive that day I thought about how so often we can look at someone and make a snap judgment on their worth by what we initially see. Such as how they dress, how they behave, or how they speak. The true treasure of a person is what's *inside*. When we take time to open the door, step inside, and look for the value in their heart. THAT'S the true treasure. Chances are good that when we take the time to discover the treasure inside someone, they will discover the treasure inside of us.

Mary treasured up all these things *and pondered them in her heart* (Luke 2:19).

Authenticity

My friend loves to thrift shop, and to her credit, she finds some of the most amazing things for the most amazing prices! Not too long ago she showed me this designer bag that she picked up for about twenty bucks from a local thrift store. The real deal would easily be worth hundreds of dollars. Looking at the outside of the bag it *looked* like a designer bag. All the signatures of that designer appeared to be in place. But, I've been tricked before. The real tell? It was the label on the *inside* of the bag. The leather label stitched perfectly inside and carefully embossed with the brand name and the following note from its maker… 'This is a _____bag. It was handcrafted from the finest materials. Its superior craftsmanship and attention to detail reflect our commitment to enduring quality.'

As I looked at that label I had a thought. What makes us authentic? We can wear designer clothes and shoes, dye away the gray, every hair in place, and look picture-perfect. We can go to church every week, carry our Bible everywhere, and utter "God bless you" to everyone we see. Does that make us authentic? We've been fooled before, haven't we? Maybe we've fooled some *ourselves,* along the way.

There's no fooling when someone gets a good look inside. No way can we be perfect or live up to the expectations of others, even worse, our own demands. But we can be real. Real, authentic people own their mistakes and shortcomings. No excuses. Authentic believers know they are loved by God and try to love others as much as others will allow. Some days may be better than others but on those not-so-good days, they don't fake it. They admit they are struggling and accept help when they need it.

Inside, I want to be loved and treasured, not for who I can pretend to be, but for who I really am. Flaws-and-all. I'm willing to bet that you are as well. The good news is that the King of the Universe, our Creator, breathed life into us. Our Maker left His mark. If you look closely you'll see it. It reads, *"This is My daughter. She was handcrafted from the finest materials. The superior craftsmanship and attention to detail reflect Our commitment to enduring quality."* His mark of authenticity is the only one that really counts. Be who He made you to be!

I will praise You, for I am fearfully and wonderfully made; Marvelous are Your works, and that my soul knows very well (Psalm 139:14 NKJV).

Indelible

I woke up thinking about this word today: *Indelible*. I often think about it in the context of ink, like a permanent marker. When I looked up the definition (in Merriam-Webster and Oxford dictionaries), I saw these words... "leaving marks that cannot be removed, unfading, enduring, unforgettable, not able to be forgotten or removed." Wow. Indelible... is forever.

People, places, and events can leave an indelible impression on us such as a parent, a father figure, your children, and your grandkids, or even a vacation spot that became a favorite getaway for you and your spouse. Other things like a tattoo, a wedding, a water baptism, a funeral, each one made a difference in one way or another. Think about it, from the moment the connection was made your life was forever changed.

The greatest indelible mark that's ever touched my life leaving a mark *so unforgettable* that it cannot be removed is God's grace in my life. Ushered in through the blood of His Son, Jesus Christ, when I said, "I believe." From the moment I said, "Yes" to Him my life changed forever.

When we are intentional in our relationships we leave an indelible mark on the lives we touch. Not that we would be remembered for anything we've done but that long after we're gone what's left behind is the indelible impression - the fingerprint of God.

> *In Him, you also, when you heard the word of truth, the good news of your salvation, and [as a result] believed in Him, were stamped with the seal of the promised Holy Spirit [the One promised by Christ] as owned and protected [by God].*
>
> Ephesians 1:13 AMP

God is making all things new

Broken Crayons

At the beginning of every school year, my mom bought me a fresh box of crayons. You may have gotten a box too. Remember? The wrappers were brand new. Perfectly fresh points to help color inside the lines. Eventually, the points wear down. The wrappers peel away. And that would make it easy to spot our favorite colors, right? They were the crayons that were most worn in the box.

We are kind of like those crayons. The more life we live, the more worn we can become. The labels we wear may get a little torn. Or we may even find ourselves feeling exposed like we are left with no covering at all.

I saw a Facebook post recently that read "Broken crayons still color." And, oh yes, they absolutely do! If you are feeling broken today, worn out, or exposed, God is making all things new! Your beautiful color still has great value. So don't give up! Keep coloring. You are part of a gorgeous tapestry that God has designed.

Do not remember the former things, nor consider the things of old. Behold I will do a new thing (Isaiah 43:18-19 NKJV).

There Is a Cost

She danced as though no one was watching... But we were. We couldn't look away.

No one else was dancing. Yet she danced in complete abandon. Face lifted toward the ceiling with a look on her face of peace and joy. Like *real joy*. She seemed so out of place because in this large group of people, no one else danced. We were singing, raising a hand occasionally to worship, but that was the farthest any of us were willing to go in our worship.

Later I learned that she had experienced such tragedy as her son was killed in a fiery car crash and she saw it happen. Unable to do anything to rescue her beloved son she was forced to surrender him to death in this life.

When I remember her and that dance of absolute abandon I am reminded that there was a cost for her kind of praise. She had experienced the depth of agony that many of us never will, yet in all of her pain, she found a way to let go, to turn her mourning and heartbreak into dancing before her King. To speak no words but, in every sway, twirl, and bow, say to her Father that she surrendered all that she knew in this world for the promise of His forever, where there are no more tears, or loss, or pain or suffering.

In the Bible, there was a woman who loved her Master so much she entered a house during a dinner party, uninvited and unwelcomed. Falling at His feet, she broke open a beautiful box made of alabaster containing a very expensive bottle of perfume, poured it over His feet and with a stream of tears, washed His feet and dried them with her hair. While the men watched and ridiculed her for wasting such a treasure, her Master's heart was moved at the depth and cost of her worship, and His love for her was so evident to everyone in the room, especially to her.

I believe that when she left His physical presence that evening, the smell of that perfume in her hair stayed with her for a very long time. A reminder that the cost of her praise brought her to a place of abandon. *Not* abandoned, but a safe place where she could *abandon* her sorrow, shame, grief, pain, and loneliness for joy, feeling valued, cherished, fulfilled, and the knowledge that she was truly loved and never really alone. The fragrance of her worship reminded her that she had been in the presence of her King and that she was adored. No doubt, that beautiful fragrance was evident to those around her as well.

No one else can truly know the depth of our pain, our loss, our shame, our grief... but Jesus. Likewise, no one will truly understand the cost of our praise, when we do the unthinkable, perhaps the unacceptable in the eyes of others. When we choose not to grow bitter and angry, but are determined to abandon it all to worship, with all that we are, the One who looks at us with a love we've never experienced before. The kind of praise that brings us into the presence of the One who whispers to our soul, "I know the cost of your praise, and your worship is beautiful and precious to Me. In this world, trouble WILL find you, but know this, I will NEVER leave you."

Radical worship will look different on every one of us. But it's only radical to the onlookers who don't know the cost of our praise. To the King, who truly knows, it is extravagantly beautiful.

"I know the cost of your praise."

I Can't Wait for You to Read This

When my beautiful granddaughter, Macey Leigh, was born I bought a Bible that I wanted to study through with the specific intention to write margin notes especially for her. Messages from my heart. Truths I want her to know. Passages I picked especially for her to read. Promises I want her to know that I have prayed *specifically* for her.

This week during a Bible study as we landed in Hebrews 7 (NKJV), my eyes fell on a note I wrote in the margin. The verses 24 and 25 were underlined and read,

> But He, because He continues forever, has an unchangeable priesthood. Therefore He is also able to save to the uttermost those who come to God through Him, since He always lives to make intercession for them.

As I turned my Bible to read the note I'd written months ago in the margin, I saw these words, "Macey — Jesus is ALWAYS praying over you! Forever." A smile broke out on my face and a delightful warmth came over me just imagining the moment she turns the pages of this precious book and sees my personal note to her. And I whispered, "I can't wait for you to read this!"

I thought about this book, The Bible; God's Word. It was physically written by men under the inspiration of God's Holy Spirit. It is not just a historical recollection of stories, genealogies, and sermons. The Bible is God's heart… written for us to find direction, be encouraged, get wisdom, and know His heart for us. It IS personal. It's the one book in all the world, in all of history, where the Author is in love with the reader. I think when His written word was completed, He joyfully smiled, thinking about the moments we would discover His heart of love for us in these pages. Can you hear His whisper… "I can't wait for you to read this!"

Coffee Dates & Losing Weight

A couple of weeks ago a beautiful couple stopped by the radio station to say hello, get a tour of the facility and meet the staff. From the moment I met Mike & Jamie, I felt a connection. I mentioned to Jamie that I'd love to have coffee with her one day and get to know her better. Before the sun had set that day we had a coffee date on the calendar!

We met yesterday. I'm thankful Starbucks doesn't charge by the hour! But I'm convinced some of the best conversations happen over the rims of mugs! And so that is one of my favorite places to chat with friends. Just as I suspected, Jamie is a beautiful person with an amazing story of grace. We talked about our families, about life and things that we may have carried around in the past that weighed us down, and what we are passionate about seeing God do through us.

As I was driving home I thought about a verse in Hebrews 10:24-25 (ESV) that reads,

> *And let us consider how to stir up one another to love and good works, not neglecting to meet together, as is the habit of some, but encouraging one another, and all the more as you see the Day drawing near.*

There's a principle in that instruction that brings great benefits. Encouraging someone else encourages us! Think about how we can stir each other up to love more, do more, and spend time together! I like to think if coffee shops were a hangout back in Biblical times… that verse might've even said… "Not neglecting to meet together at *(insert favorite coffee shop here)."*

Feeling a little down? Heavy things weighing on your heart? Call up a friend, or make a new friend and grab a cup of coffee or hot tea with them. Encourage someone and you may find that it encourages you too. I drove away feeling lighter. Chances are good that you will too!

In the Quiet

My word for this year has been "Quiet." What a beautiful year of discovery I've had this year with a word that I had actually tried to "give back" to God and exchange for a different one because... well, me... quiet?! What was He thinking?

One day, I found myself considering the differences between silence and quietness.

Silence feels cold, disconnected, empty, deafening, anxious, and, at times, hope-less.

Quietness feels warm, like I'm leaning in, expectant, waiting, anticipating something "more," like a home for peace or where peace dwells, hope-full.

While silence and quietness may sound the same to the untrained ear, the soul recognizes the difference within the environment our spirit finds itself. In silence, it chooses to give in to anxiety and worry that chokes out hope.

Isaiah 30:15: *This is what the Sovereign Lord, the Holy One of Israel, says: "In repentance and rest is your salvation, in quietness and trust is your strength."*

When we choose to wait in quietness we find ourselves actually *leaning in* to hear our Father's voice. Our soul can hear and respond to Deep calling deep. It's in that environment of quietness that peace and hope are fostered. We can find rest for our souls, even when things are chaotic and especially when life is hard. Our soul longs for quietness where we wait, expectant and anticipating His voice… and we find strength.

In the quietness, it's where we can finally breathe. And it's where we find a little taste of *home*.

Gracelaced

I know this is going to give away my age. My early teen years were during the era of sewing lace to the bottom of a dress if it was still age-appropriate but shorter than your mama and the pastor of your church deemed acceptable. I seriously remember hearing that in a sermon!

Lace also adds personality & femininity, not just to clothing, but pillows, bedding, and curtains. It makes things look softer and warmer - more inviting. When I was learning to sew… I would say lace covered a multitude of my "oops."

This morning I saw the word "gracelaced" in connection with the Proverbs 31 Woman. I don't even think it's a real word. When I googled it I didn't find it in the dictionary but I found a number of blog posts and products based around it. And I love it!

What an instant word picture I got just imagining my life *completely laced with grace!* Where patience is lacking... grace. When my heart has been hurt and I struggle with forgiving... grace. Missing sleep, lack of funds, shortness in my schedule, feeling inadequate... grace. Grace for myself and grace for others.

I know it has to be applied TO me before it can genuinely happen THROUGH me. So receiving the beautiful gift of the grace of God is where it begins. The life laced with grace is inviting, softer, and warmer. Grace speaks, sometimes even without words, that though mistakes happen we still have value. We matter. Gracelaced. I want that!

She is clothed in strength and dignity. She can laugh at the days to come. She speaks with wisdom and faithful instruction is on her tongue (Proverbs 31:25-26).

I Can Do It!

'I can do it!' she stated. Adamant. Confident. Her little 4-year-old stature was determined to do it all by herself! From the minute my beautiful little red-haired princess made her debut in this world it seems she has been determined to be independent. While it was a challenge at times when she was little - it is one of the things I admire most about her today. As a young adult, Abigail is amazing at just about everything she does. And she still wants to do it—all—by—herself!

This morning I read this verse in the Bible from 2 Corinthians 3:5. Then I opened up a devotional I've been reading and that SAME scripture was in today's reading! Whenever that happens, I take notice. I know it's definitely something God wants me to pay attention to! 2 Corinthians 3:5 reads, *Not that we are competent in ourselves to claim anything for ourselves, but our competence comes from God.*

Competence is the ability to perform a job properly and effectively; it comes from a combination of personality traits, habits, training, and experience… and our efforts are overshadowed and empowered by His Holy Spirit.

On days when you're feeling competent (you're wearing your Wonder Woman cape with your hands on your hips, your chin is lifted high and you are shouting confidently, "I can do it!") remember that it is God that enables us and works it all for His glory. Especially on the days when you feel more like the little guy in the New Testament who showed up in a crowd of hungry people carrying a couple of fish and a few loaves of bread… remember the first step is to just show up!

Show up and give Him what you have. God will use it all for His glory!

Two Bananas and a Smile

There were about a dozen of us facing each other on long bench seats in the back of a big truck. Holding onto the side of the truck while it jostled and jerked up the Dominican mountainside on a winding dirt path.

The closer we got to the top the more garbage we began to see on the sides of the road, the more flies we encountered and the worse it smelled.

The Dump—everything you can imagine and more. Piles upon piles of garbage, waste, spoiled food, and sewage. Some piles were smoking - burning below the surface from the heat. This is where the people of the villages come, about three times a week, to find something to eat or something to sell to buy food to feed their families. They walk about two miles up the mountain and spend the day foraging. If they can fill a recycled burlap bag with bottles they will carry it down a big hill on the other side to a recycling center at the entrance where they will earn about five pesos for the entire bag. That's about two and a half cents for their *whole days'* labor.

Right after we arrived a local man, who makes several five-gallon buckets full of soup every day, pulled up behind us. He also brings a tank of water for them to fill whatever jug they may have to drink and carry back home.

I watched a woman pick through a pile of garbage to find a dirty 2-liter soda bottle. She unscrewed the top, sniffed inside it, and walked over to fill it up with water. She drank some and filled it up again. I swallowed hard. Our eyes connected over a cup of soup and what I saw surprised me: Resilience, Hope, Life.

Many would not leave their piles to come for the soup. We carried cups of soup out to them throughout the dump. But! When the man went back to the cab of his truck and brought out the bananas… *everyone* came! They were each allowed TWO bananas. And they waited in lines for them. We spoke English. They spoke Spanish and some Creole but we all found common ground that day over two bananas… and a smile. I'm convinced it's the international sign for kindness.

Hot, tired, and emotionally spent, we loaded up the truck and made the trek down to the bottom of the mountain and back through the town of Sosua. All through the town the locals waved and smiled and hollered "hola" to us. Their lives are hard. Life is dangerous. It is a struggle to survive every single day. But within the struggle, they have a simple cadence to life. Family is everything and time is told by the rising and the setting of the sun.

That day, as we headed back to Sosua, to our air-conditioned rooms, to shower and meet back up for an amazing buffet of Dominican food by the beautiful waterside, I heard God whisper these words... "Privilege comes with a price." I don't know why God chose to put me here in America and put that beautiful lady, in a little village beside a garbage dump, but I know that God has given each of us gifts, talents, knowledge, time, and, yes, treasure to use for His Kingdom.

So when we can give bananas, *give* bananas. When we can sponsor a child for an education and a hot meal to break the cycle of poverty—we must! When we can go there to serve like Jesus—we must! It will bless them and it will change us... forever!

> *If God has been generous with you, He will expect you to serve Him well. But if He has been more than generous, He will expect you to serve Him even better.*
>
> Luke 12:48 CEV

God has given each of us treasure to use for His Kingdom

Come and See

Usually, the first word my brain can make out when my alarm goes off at 4 am is "coffee." This morning it was "Psalm 46."

I grabbed my coffee and headed to the studio and I opened my journal to jot down a few thoughts. The verse on the page was from Psalm 46, the subtitle read, "For the director of music. A song." So you may not know what I do at The Bridge (the radio station where I work) when I'm not in the studio, I program the music. Part of that is selecting the music that is played on the air. I already knew I MUST pay attention to this conversation that God and I were nuancing this morning before the sun was even up.

God is our refuge and strength, an ever-present help in trouble. Therefore, we will not fear... God is within her, she will not fall; God will help her at break of day. (Trust me, when the mic opens at 6:08 every morning THAT IS my prayer!)

Come and see what the Lord has done. (The most simple way to share my faith… no hype, no deep theology… just a simple invitation from my heart to yours… to come and see what He has done for me and what He can do for you….)

And finally… *He says, 'Be still and know that I am God' …The Lord Almighty is with us and He is our fortress.*

I'm not always such an intent listener. But I'm really thankful today that I listened to hear His heart for me… for us. How much He wants to meet with us if we'll listen.

Come and see….

what you see determines what you do

Where You Sit

I heard a statement in church Sunday that resonated with me. "Where you sit determines what you see, and what you see determines what you do."

Come and sit with Jesus for a few minutes this morning. Ask for wisdom and to be able to see through His eyes what is before you today. You can react to the worries and stresses of this day out of fear or you can *choose* to shut out the chaotic noise and focus on His voice. Hear His voice that says, *Do not fear (anything), for I am with you* (Isaiah 41:10 AMP).

It starts with where you choose to sit. Where you sit determines what you see and what you see determines what you do.

Inspector 25

This morning as I was getting dressed I noticed a small white circular sticker stuck to my knee with the number 25 on it. I knew it had come off of the inside of the new pj's I'd worn all night and was now stuck on me.

Those pj's had been inspected by "Inspector number 25." Who was that anonymous person? How many inspectors are there? Are all their standards the same? Is that the occupation they claim on their tax return?... Inspector 25.

Immediately I had this thought... I'm so thankful I know my inspector *personally*. Intricately formed. Creatively crafted. The Psalmist said we are fearfully and wonderfully made, and we are completely known by our Master Designer.

If we could see the tag on the inside of our soul it would read, *Made in the Image of God*; and when we receive the good news that we are saved through Christ, we receive His special seal. There is no number because there is only One who gets to do the final inspection and put His seal on us.

You heard and believed the message of truth, the Good News that He has saved you. In Him, you were sealed with the Holy Spirit whom He promised (Ephesians 1:13 GNT).

All In!

The last of the decorations had been put away for another year. As I was storing them, I remembered a Christmas past when my two-year-old granddaughter was opening her presents. The very last thing she opened was a little pop-up princess tent. We put it on the floor and opened the flap trying to coax her into crawling inside but for some reason, she was too scared to go in. No matter how hard we tried to convince her, she was NOT going to crawl into that tent!

Finally, her daddy picked up the tent and dropped it over the top of his head and shoulders while he was sitting on the sofa. So the flap was right at eye level for her to see inside. Once she saw her daddy inside — she was ALL IN! She crawled inside right into his lap, giggling and unafraid.

We've all been there, haven't we? Too afraid to move into a new place; missing out on something new that God has for us because it's unknown. When we realize that our Father, God, is *already there* beckoning us to go ALL IN! We are not alone and we can trust Him, we can trade our fear for a bold faith that wherever God leads us, He will go with us.

You who sit down in the High God's presence, spend the night in Shaddai's shadow. Say this: 'God, You're my refuge. I trust in You and I'm safe!' (Psalm 91:1-2 MSG).

Stay Where I Can See You

When my kiddos got old enough that I could let them play in the backyard for a while by themselves I would tell them, "Stay where I can see you!" I might be folding laundry or washing dishes, but I was able to glance out of the kitchen window or the back patio and keep an eye on them. Of course, I wanted to keep them out of trouble but I also wanted trouble to stay away from them and I wanted them to learn to follow directions.

Sometimes they got interested in something beyond the backyard and would go beyond where I could see them. I would then go find them and bring them back. When they got into something they knew they weren't supposed to get into... they would hide. As a parent, we know that is a sure sign they are up to something!

That's nothing new. We don't have to read very far into the Bible to find people hiding. Adam and Eve, Elijah, and Jonah were hiding for a variety of reasons... but none could hide from God, and neither can we. There's a great benefit of staying where God has us. It's not that we could hide from God. The benefit is OURS when we stay where we can see HIM!

Psalm 139: 7-10 (CEV) reminds us that He is always with us!

> *Where could I go to escape from Your Spirit or from Your sight? If I were to climb up to the highest heavens, You would be there. If I were to dig down to the world of the dead You would also be there. Suppose I had wings like the dawning day and flew across the ocean. Even then Your powerful arm would guide and protect me.*

So it's not about staying where God can see us. Let's determine today that we are going to stay where we can see HIM!

from Him comes my hope

Airplane Mode

If you've ever boarded an airplane you know that part of the pre-flight instruction to all passengers is that you must put your cell phone in airplane mode. That setting on your phone disables all of the Bluetooth, wi-fi, cellular, and data connections on your mobile device. The reason is that nothing onboard interferes with the airplane's sensors and equipment.

Usually, the first thing every passenger does once we've landed is turn off airplane mode. Ever notice the buzzing and dinging that can be heard all over the plane as messages, missed calls, calendar notes, and other notifications all come through? So much information, some important and some distractions compelling us to pay attention.

What if we purposed to spend some time every day in airplane mode? It's not just the phone. TV, social media, email, and even conversations at times. It's the constant humming and buzzing of information that our brain is constantly trying to take in and file… somewhere… it can be overwhelming! It can definitely hinder us from hearing that still, small voice that calls us to a deeper conversation with our Maker.

My soul, be quiet before God, for from Him comes my hope (Psalm 62:5 ISV).

Are you struggling with hopelessness? Feeling overwhelmed? Do you need peace today? Switching to airplane mode to have a conversation with God is a good place to begin.

Just Stay Calm

One of my favorite promises in the Bible is this: *The Lord Himself will fight for you. Just stay calm.* And wow! Did God fight for His people! The story in Exodus 14 is packed full of drama, mystery, and miracles! It's the story of the Red Sea and about a million of God's people walking on dry ground between two incredibly gigantic walls of water as God held back the sea to rescue the Israelites.

Oh there was a LOT of celebrating on the other side of the Red Sea once they saw what God did to save them. But what were they doing BEFORE the answer arrived? Pretty much freaking out! Complaining and wishing they could go back to Egypt where they'd been enslaved and abused. Not one of their finest moments, to be sure.

If we are being honest, we've all been there. That "Red Sea" moment when we thought God was leading us in a direction and all of a sudden the enemy came rushing in. Whatever it is… or was… it felt like life or death. What God did for His people in Exodus 14 is a reminder of what He will do for us now.

Moses told the people in Exodus 14:13-14:

> *Don't be afraid. Just stand still and watch the Lord rescue you today. The Egyptians you see today will never be seen again. The Lord Himself will fight for you. Just stay calm.*

What if we choose to worship God - in front of the Red Sea? BEFORE we can see the outcome… what if we trust Him… and instead of worrying we choose to thank Him for His provision AHEAD of the storm! God gives us that direction. We can pray God's Word in confidence and expectation, like this: I will not be afraid! Lord, I am going to stand still and watch You rescue me today. Thank you that You, God, are fighting for me! And in that, I can just remain calm.

Collecting What's Important

I love to collect certain things. If I love them and they bring me joy... why not? I remember buying my first Longaberger basket. Pretty. Functional. Valuable. I LOVED it! And I decided to buy more - thinking the value would only increase and I could pass them down to my children.

Well, I now have quite a collection of functional, not-so-valuable baskets *and* my daughter has ZERO interest in inheriting my collection! I understand. She didn't live through the era of brass tags and limited edition collecting and hostess credits. And honestly, they are a BEAST to keep dusted!

We all tend to collect things. Either for pleasure or sentimentality, things become valuable to us. But nothing compares to the treasures we must be focused on storing up in heaven. There are no baskets, jewelry, artwork, or baseball cards. There's nothing wrong with those things, but they can't be our priority.

Don't keep hoarding for yourselves earthly treasures that can be stolen by thieves. Material wealth eventually rusts, decays, and loses its value. Instead, stockpile heavenly treasures for yourselves that cannot be stolen and will never rust, decay, or lose their value. For your heart will always pursue what you esteem as your treasure.
Matthew 6:19-21 TPT

Your heart will always pursue what you esteem as your treasure. Wow! Heavenly treasures. If you are hearing my voice or reading this now, YOU are Heaven's greatest treasure. That Jesus lived a sinless life here on earth, bore all of our sins on the cross, died and rose up to live again is how you and I can live forever in heaven!! Sharing His story with as many who will listen and believe… now THAT is stockpiling heavenly treasures that can *never* be stolen!

Unlikely Company

I watched a tender video of a dad brushing his little girl's hair as she was sobbing. When he asks her what's wrong she chokes out, "I don't know." So he sweetly asks her if she'd like something special done with her hair. He was so patient with her as she finally said, still in tears, "Curls." While he plugs in the curling iron he smiles and says, "Wanna hear a joke?" He tells her a dad joke... and instantly she erupts in laughter. There's been more than half a million views of that little video that captured a dad being a heroic #GirlDad and, ok, maybe dad jokes *do* serve a purpose.

Do you ever have days like that little one? You just feel blue. Maybe there IS someone or something that you're carrying grief over. Sometimes there is just no explanation. There's just a sadness that hangs like a cloud over your heart. Proverbs 14:13 (NLT) tells us, *Laughter can conceal a heavy heart, but when the laughter ends, the grief remains.*

My family and I are closing in on the first anniversary of the loss of my brother. We've nearly experienced all the firsts in this first year of living without him. My sister-in-love and I were talking this past week about how we were feeling about this milestone. It is hard to put it into words. On his birthday I wrote it this way, "I'm not sorry that you're there. I'm just sad that you're not here."

Maybe you can relate. Grief has so many layers and as we go through the process we find things to smile about… maybe even laugh out loud over. I believe that verse is less about what to do or not do, and more to confirm that in this life there will be heartache, but it is ok to find moments of laughter… even joy. And that it's alright to keep company with grief and joy side by side. We can be sure of this when we are finding our way through those days, we are not alone. God promised that, *The Lord is near to the brokenhearted and saves the crushed in spirit* (Psalm 34:18 ESV). And *that* is the BEST company to keep!

The Unforced Rhythms of Grace

"Are you tired? Worn out? Burned out on religion? Come to me. Get away with me and you'll recover your life. I'll show you how to take a real rest. Walk with me and work with me—watch how I do it. Learn the unforced rhythms of grace. I won't lay anything heavy or ill-fitting on you. Keep company with me and you'll learn to live freely and lightly."
Matthew 11:28-30 MSG

Jesus spoke that invitation to His disciples and followers as a beautiful offer of exchange to us all. Bring Him *all* that is weighing us down, causing us pain, keeping us up at night, and keeping us from truly connecting with our Father and He will take it on. In exchange, He will teach us what real rest feels like.

Learning by example is always easier than trying to figure things out on our own. Jesus offers to walk with Him and work with Him and watch how He does it… and that offer is good today. The beauty of that unforced rhythm of grace is that we respond to His invitation, not out of obligation but out of desiring a relationship. Evangelist Joseph Prince said it this way: "The reality is, when you don't read the Bible, you should not be feeling guilty; you should be feeling *hungry*."

You can be sure of this: when we mess up and it's inevitable that we will, we don't have to hide. Jesus began with our exhaustion and disillusion and said - bring it! No matter what it is or how often we find ourselves way in over our heads, bring it all to Him. Jesus said,*"Keep company with Me and you will learn to live freely and lightly"* (Matthew 11:30 MSG).

Right now is the perfect time to lighten your load and follow His beautiful rhythm of grace!

The Old Orange Jar

I made a last-minute impulse buy when I was redecorating my daughter's bedroom a few years ago. On the way to the register my eyes fell on this gallon-sized ceramic jar. It had shapes cut out on the sides and it was orange. I don't know what made me do it, not even sure what I was going to use it for in her room… but I bought it.

Today, my daughter's room is no longer that theme, but I can not part with that orange ceramic jar. Last year I discovered that the opening was just the right size to drop a candle down inside and wow! It's still an old orange jar with holes in the sides; but, in the dark, the light glowing through those cutouts on the sides is beautiful!

You and I are sort of like that orange ceramic jar. Fragile, and unique, and some of us may have more holes from wounds we've weathered than others. But, unlike my last-minute impulse buy, we've been chosen by the Master Potter for a very specific and spectacular mission in this world... to carry the Light! 2 Corinthians 4:7 (MSG) says:

> If you only look at us, you might well miss the brightness. We carry this precious Message around in the unadorned clay pots of our ordinary lives. That's to prevent anyone from confusing God's incomparable power with us.

The next time you're feeling like the old clay pot, focus on the One we get to carry around in our hearts to share with the world. What a privilege we have been given to carry the Light!

YOU ARE SPEEDING!

We've all seen those radar speed signs typically in residential areas that flash your current speed up as you approach it. If it begins flashing your speed it's meant to be a reminder of the current speed and to slow it down.

One day as I was driving through the town I live in, I was deep in thought, which usually gets me into trouble. All of a sudden I rounded the corner and the radar sign didn't flash my speed. It did something I had never seen before... and have never seen since. In bright yellow CAPITAL letters it screamed YOU ARE SPEEDING! Woah! Now that *definitely got my attention.* To this day I remember exactly where it happened and how quickly I reduced my speed!

One of the most valuable gifts God has given us as believers is His Holy Spirit living inside us. He gives us wisdom and discernment. He helps us stay on track. When we are approaching a potentially dangerous situation He can warn us just as suddenly and intensely as that radar speed sign. Jesus knew that in this crazy world we live in, we would need the Holy Spirit. So He asked God to send Him to us!

Jesus said in John 14:16 (NLT), *"I will ask the Father, and He will give you another Advocate, who will never leave you."* In Greek, the word Advocate is "Paraclete" which also means Comforter, Encourager, and Counselor. It is definitely to our advantage to pay attention to His direction!

Generous Giving, Generous Living

I grew up going to church. We went to Bible study every Wednesday night and to church TWICE on Sundays. Wherever there was a church service, an offering plate or bucket was being passed. The one thing I remember hearing almost every time… "you can't out-give God;" in my lifetime I have certainly found that to be true!

That principle is not only true in what we would call our "treasure," it is also true in our "time" and "talent." Whatever the gifts or talents we have been given, whether it is the ability to grow, to build, to make music, to write, or to bake….or maybe it is the gift of time… having coffee with a friend and listening while they unload some of their heavy heart, you cannot out-give what God has poured into you and continues to every day.

2 Corinthians 9:8 (NLT) tells us, *And God will generously provide all you need, then you will always have everything you need and plenty left over to share with others.*

Being generous with what we do have opens the door for God to pour even more into our lives. When we live a life of generous giving with our time, talents, and treasure that is when we look the most like our Heavenly Father. It is true, we cannot out-give God. But what would our family, our church, our workplace and our community be like if we tried?

What's In a Nap?

Isn't it absolute irony that when we are young our parents insist that we need a nap and we will try just about anything to get out of taking one? Then we grow up, have a lot of responsibilities and we *wish* we could just take a nap! Eventually, we get to the age that we *absolutely* love taking a bit of a siesta! Maybe it's a rite of passage? I think it's exhausting to juggle all that we do. It's not all physical workload that drains us. We tend to carry a lot of stuff around on our hearts, in our minds, within our souls... it makes us weary from the inside out. That is why I love what the prophet Isaiah said in his 40th chapter. He was specifically mentioning those of us who feel lost in the shuffle of life... insignificant in the race we're running, wondering... does God really see me?

God doesn't come and go. God lasts. He's Creator of all you can see or imagine. He doesn't get tired out, doesn't pause to catch His breath. And He knows everything, inside and out. He energizes those who get tired, gives fresh strength to dropouts. For even young people tire and drop out, young folk in their prime stumble and fall. But those who wait upon God get fresh strength. They spread their wings and soar like eagles. They run and don't get tired. They walk and don't lag behind.

Isaiah 40:29-31 MSG

It's not a nap that most of us need. We *need* to spend time and attention with the God who lasts. When we do, He promises fresh strength. I would love that today. How about you?

In the Waiting

> *I waited and waited and waited some more, patiently, knowing God would come through for me. Then, at last, He bent down and listened to my cry.*
>
> Psalm 40:1 TPT

Are you there yet? I mean...at the waiting and waiting and waiting some more... part. Life is hard. Days are long. Friends are not always friendly and betrayals cut so deep we don't know if we'll survive.

Waiting for God to come through for us is tough to do. We live in an instant gratification world. Waiting when we know He could swoop in and fix it right now is frustrating and painful. But, His timetable always includes what is the absolute best plan for our lives. What we learn in the waiting teaches us far more than we could ever learn if everything came easy and quick. Sometimes, it's just about "learning to be patient" that keeps us waiting. While other times, the wait is part of a much larger plan that impacts more than just us and God knows exactly when the answer must come.

Either way, while we are waiting, we can trust that God *will* lean in. He *will* hear our cry. When I find myself waiting and waiting on God to move in an area of my life, my prayer becomes, "Lord, what do You want me to learn in this waiting? How can I serve You in the meantime? I know that You will come through for me, however that looks in Your plan. Thank You for hearing my heart today, God. I will wait until I hear You say, 'It's time!'"

He will hear our cry

Casting

My experience with fishing is very limited. I think I can count on one hand the number of times I've gone fishing. So much waiting... so much quiet are my top reasons for not having my own rod and reel. Followed quickly by the whole idea of unhooking whatever I finally caught. Mmm hmmm— *not* my idea of relaxing. But one thing I think of every time I remember my Fishing 101 lesson? Remembering to *unlock* the fishing line *before* I cast out the line!

When I forgot to release the line, I would swing the pole as hard as I could and that line never left my reel! Embarrassing? Yes! Did I ever forget again? No! Releasing the lock on my reel allowed my swing to cast that line with the hook and the bait way out away from me and drop it in the water.

When I read Psalm 55:22 the word "cast" reminds me of my few fishing experiences. This Bible verse gives us instruction AND a promise when we obey. It reads, *Cast your cares on the LORD and He will sustain you; He will never let the righteous be shaken.*

Some Bible translations say, "leave your troubles," or "tell your worries," but I LOVE that visual of casting. We need to remember to UNLOCK the line and CAST whatever worry or burden, fear or frustration onto the One who tells us to do it. Don't just drop it. It's too easy to pick it back up! Cast it. Let it go!

God knows we are weary. He knows we could bend and falter beneath the weight of all we try to carry ourselves. When we follow His instructions, God promises to sustain us. He will never let the righteous be shaken. Are you in need of support to keep going? Do you feel like your world is being shaken? Go back to the instruction of Psalm 55:22. Begin by unlocking the line you've kept tethered to you with all your cares attached… and cast it all on Him.

Having a Spotter

Do you know what a "spotter" is? Maybe the better question is, do you know the importance of *having* a spotter? Wikipedia says, "Spotting in weight or resistance training is the act of supporting another person during a particular exercise, with an emphasis on allowing the participant to lift or push more than they could normally do safely. Correct spotting involves knowing when to intervene and assist with a lift, and encouraging a training partner to push beyond the point in which they would normally return the weight to its stationary position."

That's what we need some days, don't we?! What if we had someone walking around with us every day who spoke words of affirmation like, "You can do this!" "You are enough!" "You are loved!"? Someone who pointed out the "Lift here - not there." One who encouraged us to keep at the hard things and jumped in to help when we were trying to pick up and carry around a weight that was too much for us.

I have really good news for you today, the Holy Spirit is with us, 24/7. There are some weights we must carry in this life but God already knows what we are capable of when we are fully equipped with His Spirit. Likewise, there are some weights we were never meant to carry and because of Jesus' sacrifice, we can lay them down.

I love how *The Passion Translation* paraphrases 1 Corinthians 10:13:

> *We all experience times of testing, which is normal for every human being. But God will be faithful to you. He will screen and filter the severity, nature, and timing for every test or trial you face so that you can bear it.*

The Holy Spirit is like a spotter... and oh so much more! If you haven't started working out with Him yet... be aware of His presence with you... today is your day!

Lessons from a Toddler

There is nothing quite like trying to dress a toddler. Their energy knows no bounds. Their little minds are constantly thinking - what's next? Where can I go? Ooo what's up there? Hey, what's this, and what does it do? The creativity and interest level of a toddler is pretty incredible. With very little thought for danger, a toddler is driven largely by curiosity and experience.

Saying "Wait" to a toddler... well, if you've had one or taken care of one, you know it doesn't mean much to them. It's in those earliest discovery moments that we begin to teach children about safety and obedience and the consequences of our actions.

Even as adults we struggle with the concept of waiting. Psalm 27:14 teaches us an important component of waiting. It tells us what to DO while we wait: *Wait for the Lord; be strong and take heart and wait for the Lord.*

While we are waiting we are to be strong, encouraged, to have hope, to be bold and confident… to not give up! There is a LOT of doing in that one little verse of instruction.

I think if we could bottle up any of that toddler energy and curiosity we could serve it up best right here… in the waiting… in the watching expectantly for the goodness of God and just how He will reveal His greatness in our lives. Now THAT is curiosity and wonder put to good use… while we are waiting!

Under Pressure

When I visited the Dominican Republic a couple of years ago, I met a street vendor who was selling jewelry that had the prettiest blue stones in it. The stone is called Larimar or blue Pectolite and is an extremely rare gemstone. It has been found only in one location: a mountainous, relatively inaccessible area in the Dominican Republic.

I picked out a few pieces to bring home as gifts and as the vendor was wrapping them for me he handed me a piece of dull brownish stone that had just a bit of blue showing and said, "That is what it looks like before it is ground and polished." The difference between them was stunning. Without the grinding and polishing that stone looked unremarkable and of little value.

I am reminded of the process of life we go through when we are tested. Every test gives us an opportunity to allow our faith to go through the grinding and polishing. It is how we learn the faithfulness and goodness of God. It is what gives us the opportunity to choose faith over fear and sometimes without even realizing it our faith in God becomes a beautiful reminder to others that they can trust in Him too.

You know that under pressure, your faith-life is forced into the open and shows its true colors (James 1:3 MSG).

Only God knows what lies beneath the rough, muted exterior of our heart. Trusting the Master's hand at grinding and polishing with just the right amount of pressure will produce the most glorious colors and the end result will be worth it!

Tyranny of the Urgent

My to-do list often contains things that I do every day. Some are work related and some are personal. I know that I'm going to need to do them and I would do them without a reminder. But, I put them on the list partly for the satisfaction of checking them off and mostly for the reminder that they are important, even necessary. Because some days get crazy and things happen. We get pulled in a LOT of directions.

In the 1960s, a guy named Charles Hummel wrote a booklet called *The Tyranny of the Urgent*. It is all about what is important and what is urgent. There is a tension in each day of our lives between the important things that *need* to be done and the urgent matters that crop up and scream for our attention and our immediate action. Often, the important things get overlooked for the emergencies. And not all of these emergencies are true emergencies. Oh, they may be urgent matters but not always meant to be MY urgent matters. Knowing the differences and how to manage them in our lives requires prayer for wisdom and discernment from God.

I'm wondering what could be different in our lives if we put a few declarations from God's Word on our To Do list… not because they are tasks… but to serve as reminders of the IMPORTANT things in our day, so that they are not squeezed out by the urgent.

Here's an example, what if we put Psalm 59:16 at the top of our to-do list for today? *I will sing of Your strength, in the morning I will sing of Your love; for You are my fortress, my refuge in times of trouble.*

Today I WILL sing because You love me, God. Your strength and Your love are a fortress where I can feel safe and when I encounter trouble TODAY — I will take refuge in YOU. Now THAT is something to sing about! Placing it high on our list of *important things* to focus on will prepare us for urgent matters.

Part Three

Refreshment

This past weekend my family and I went to an outdoor event that we had been planning to attend for several months. We were so excited to go! Until we heard how HOT it was going to be. To be completely honest, if we hadn't already bought tickets to go, we probably would not have gone. But we committed to participate. We bought the tickets, and so we went. The heat was brutal. But the show was spectacular! And we made memories that day that we will remember LONG after the sunburn has gone away.

It's a little bit like life. We're committed. We don't always get the luxury of a heat index warning. Sometimes we are thrown into the fire and it is brutal! But on the other side of the spectrum life is also beautiful. Spectacular even! All of it...together, God uses in His plan for our lives. And He is more aware than even we are, how brutal, heated, and devastating some days are for us. And how much we need to be rejuvenated.

He refreshes my soul. He guides me along the right paths for His name's sake (Psalm 23:3).

That day, nothing felt better than a cold glass of water and a hot shower when I got home. I felt like a new person! And there are things we go through in life that can only be redeemed in our lives by the refreshing that *only* God can bring. *The Living Bible* paraphrases Psalm 23:3 this way, *He lets me rest in the meadow grass and leads me beside the quiet streams. He gives me new strength. He helps me do what honors Him the most.*

Sometimes life is hard. But trying to escape or ignore it can keep us from the incredible refreshing that God has waiting for us. Today I am grateful that God refreshes our souls. He gives us new strength. And He will help us do what honors Him the most!

Put Your Oxygen Mask on First

If you have ever flown in a commercial airplane you know that part of the emergency preparedness instructions from flight attendants is that if cabin pressure should change, an oxygen mask will drop down in front of you - and you must put *your* oxygen mask on *first*. Then assist others around you. It seems counterintuitive - especially if you are a parent traveling with a small child. You would instinctively want to put your life on the line to save your child and put their mask on first, right?

The truth is we can not save anyone if we don't take care of ourselves, first. Just as putting our own oxygen mask on first enables us to be able to help others put their masks on. We must be filling up our mind, spirit & soul with God's Word and spending time in His presence before we can share it with others around us.

The only thing that will be in heaven that we are able to take with us is the *people* that we helped in some way to find Christ. Maybe that is why Jesus began His teaching on the mountainside in Matthew 5 (NLT) with this instruction: *God blesses those who are poor and realize their need for Him, for the Kingdom of Heaven is theirs.*

When we realize we are nothing without Him and we begin to breathe in Christ, we can help others to do the same. In the spirit realm, Jesus Christ *is* our oxygen. Without Him, there is no life. How amazing it will be to enter the Kingdom of Heaven and find ourselves surrounded by those who helped us to come to Christ along with those we helped as well.

What if we began each morning by putting on our oxygen mask, breathing Jesus into every fiber of our being, so that we are ready and able to help assist others in breathing Him in as well?!

The Gift of Rest

"I will give you rest." I kept hearing that over and over while I was lying in the hospital bed. That promise that Jesus spoke in Matthew 11:28 was the verse that God whispered to me at the beginning of that year when I learned that my word for the year was going to be "REST." He's been teaching me a lot about rest but this particular lesson has been a difficult one for me.

More sick than I've ever been in my life, I found myself unable to focus on anything but the fight to survive. Prayers were short but frequent. Different Bible verses that have been embedded in my memory would come to my mind and became part of my ongoing conversations with God. Thank You Lord that Your name *is a strong tower. The righteous run into it and are safe* (Proverbs 18:10). *Those who live in the shelter of the Most High will find rest in the shadow of the Almighty* (Psalm 91:1). *I look up to the mountains - does my help come from there? My help comes from the Lord, the Maker of the heavens and the earth* (Psalm 121:1).

And this one: *Come to Me, all you who are weary and heavy burdened... and I will give you rest* (Matthew 11:28). Weary? Definitely. Heavy burdened? Absolutely! And the exchange Jesus offers? To bring it all to Him for the gift... of *rest*. Rest doesn't always feel like a gift. But when you find yourself so weary you can hardly move, carrying so much you can hardly think straight, rest is a most beautiful gift.

Rest doesn't come unaccompanied. Rest comes with peace, with healing, with the companionship of Christ and so much more. Rest for your soul brings wholeness and that is something Jesus longs to give us.

The One Whom Jesus Loved

The song "Jesus Loves Me," is still one of my favorite songs. It was a regular nightly bedtime song with my kids and now my granddaughter as well. I listen to Christian music every day that is filled with the message that Jesus loves us. I'm so thankful as I know there are many in this world who haven't heard that message that they are loved by God.

You don't have to read very far into the Bible's gospels to see that Jesus loved His disciples and those who followed Him. In fact, Jesus' love for the world was so incredibly powerful that He was committed to love each one *regardless* of their love or hatred of Him.

I was thinking of the term of endearment "the disciple whom Jesus loved" the other day. I've read those verses in John's gospel so often and thought at times that John and Jesus must have had an extraordinarily close relationship for that to have been said about John. I've wondered if the other disciples were ever jealous to think that Jesus loved John more. So as I looked up all the references to "the one whom Jesus loved," (John 13:23; 19:26; 20:2; 21:7, 20) I realized they were ALL written by John.

All of those Bible verses that called John "the disciple whom Jesus loved" were in the book of John... written BY John. Boastful? I don't think so. Teacher and author, John Piper wrote:

> Perhaps this is John's way of saying, 'My most important identity is not my name but my being loved by Jesus the Son of God.' He's not trying to rob anybody else of this privilege; he is simply exulting in it: 'I'm loved, I'm loved, I'm loved — that's who I am. I'm loved by Jesus.'*

What if we began to write that phrase about ourselves on the pages of our journal, our calendars, how about the home screen of our phone and computer? Your name... and these five words: *The one whom Jesus loves*. Would that begin to change how we love ourselves, and how we love each other? Do we truly walk in the understanding that we are loved by Jesus?

Where can you write those words today about yourself? Your name, followed by these words, the one whom Jesus loves. Because it is true. You are loved!

---

*John Piper is the founder and teacher of desiringGod.org and chancellor of Bethlehem College & Seminary. For 33 years, he served as pastor of Bethlehem Baptist Church, Minneapolis, Minnesota. He is the author of more than 50 books.

Just a Little T-L-C

I haven't had much success with plants over the years. Usually, within a few months it becomes obvious that my thumb is not green. Different plants need varying amounts of sunlight and water. I have never taken the time to learn that detail. Until I inherited a small tree planter when I moved into my office. Hidden between the desk and wall was a two-foot tree stalk that had two branches with a few leaves and what I call a dead end. It looked like a branch had been growing there but was completely cut off and nothing ever grew back.

My first thought was that I was pretty sure it was doomed, given my past experience with live plants. But a funny thing happened. I sat it up on my desk for a couple of days while my office was being painted and I noticed that in just that short amount of time, the plant actually looked a little greener.

So I named it "Hank" and I moved it over by my office window. I made Mondays my "Water Hank Day." One of my co-workers came in every morning and started telling Hank how much better he looked. So I started talking to Hank. And Hank started growing like *crazy*. More and more growth on those original branches were happening. And then, that dead end that I mentioned, began to sprout a new shoot!

Attention and care was all Hank needed to come to life. Today, Hank is thriving and probably needs to be repotted, although that may be beyond my capabilities. Attention and care. Isn't that what we all need?! Is there someone in your purview that God is tugging at your heart to speak to, to encourage, to nudge into the light, or to water a bit with the Living Word?

1 Thessalonians 5:11 (MSG) gives us the life-giving care instructions:

> *So speak encouraging words to one another. Build up hope so you'll all be together in this, no one left out, no one left behind. I know you're already doing this; just keep on doing it.*

Sneak Attacks

The military air show that we went to earlier this summer was astounding! So much pride welled up in me as we watched the skill, precision, and might of the United States Armed Forces. The men and women who train and serve our country to keep us safe and preserve our freedoms are the best in the world! We are truly grateful for their service.

The weather that day was extreme. One of the hottest days with the highest humidity of the entire summer. Being out on the tarmac made it even more grueling. We started walking toward the parking lot about an hour before the show ended just as the Thunderbirds were beginning their part of the show. The pilots were so incredibly sharp that we couldn't help but stop along the way back to our vehicle to watch this magnificent show! At one point my son, Cody, and I sat on the cement half-wall set up along the parking lot perimeter and turned toward the flight line to watch the fly by.

We felt the wind of it before we saw it or heard it. A jet flying extremely low raced over our heads... from behind, and yes, we both ducked! By the time the sound and sight of that jet hit us, it was already over us... and that is how capable they are of sneaking up on an enemy. Overtaken before they even know what has them!

I've thought of that experience a number of times since then. The Bible warns us that we have an enemy that is just that capable of a sneak attack. 1 Peter 5:8 (CEV) warns us, *Be on your guard and stay awake. Your enemy, the devil, is like a roaring lion, sneaking around to find someone to attack.* That day at the air show we were hot, dehydrated, and worn out. We were so busy watching something that was far away that we missed something right on top of us.

Stay alert. Our enemy is not flesh and blood. Our enemy is the enemy of our soul. This fight is the fight of our life! The good news… this enemy has *already* been defeated! So today we call on Jesus to walk beside, behind, before, and above. Regardless of our condition going into this day, well rested, hydrated, alert or weary and undone… we need the Lord with us! He will help us stay alert and on guard.

Safe Harbor

I was visiting a friend in Sarasota, Florida, several years ago. She and her family owned a beautiful boat that was docked in a marina filled with beautiful boats. It was interesting to me to see people spend a LOT of time on their boats, soaking up the sun, and eating meals on them. Some people were having dinner parties on their boat as the sun was setting. But I was surprised to see how few of the boats left the marina and made their way for the open water.

One of my favorite things to see is a sailboat with its sails up, being carried by the wind, and its passengers enjoying the journey. There is something so majestic about it, watching it glide along the water being carried along by the wind or resting for a while enjoying the sun, the seagulls, and the sounds of the white caps. Peaceful.

We know it is not without danger. I learned firsthand how quickly a storm can sneak up on you when you are out at sea. It is important to have a captain who knows exactly how to handle the boat, to weather the storm, and get you safely back to the harbor. It is then that we most appreciate a safe harbor. But here's the thing: boats weren't made to stay in the harbor. They were made to sail the wide open waters. With proper safety equipment and an experienced captain at the helm, a boat can do what it was created to do for an audience to enjoy the journey.

We may feel safe tied to a dock in a harbor but we weren't made to live there either. "Living our life to the full" means getting out into some uncharted areas sometimes. Jesus - the Life Giver - is the best life jacket we can wear in life. Mark 4:39 (CEV) tells us, *Jesus got up and ordered the wind and the waves to be quiet. The wind stopped, and everything was calm.*

The Holy Spirit gives us discernment to navigate the path. Trust that God is at the helm of our boat and that gives us a full crew for this journey. When was the last time you put your sails up and trusted that God was in the wind?

Judging Covers

Never judge a book by its cover. It's one of those sayings that you probably heard growing up just like I did. Despite being told that over and over we still do it, don't we? Not long ago I was in a drive-thru lane and I found myself thinking about the person in the vehicle ahead of me based on the stickers on the back of their bumper.

I think it's interesting that we can feel an emotion, both good or bad, toward a stranger just by seeing a bumper sticker on their car. Sports teams we love or dislike. Political candidates, we support or oppose. School names and favorite vacation spots. Even the little stick figures that represent our family members and pets say something about us.

Likewise, people can judge *us* and often do, by only what *they* can see, what clothes we wear, and the car we drive. We all do it. Snap decisions based on very little information. 1 Samuel 16:7 sums it up: *People look at the outward appearance, but the Lord looks at the heart.*

My prayer is that God would help me to see others through His eyes. That I would reject the quick temptation to judge by what I see. I pray that God would help us to choose to love like Jesus and leave the judging to God. One of the many things I love about what happens the more that we love like Jesus… the more others want to know the One who IS Love.

What Kind of Morning Is It?

Some days we feel like we are on top of the world! Everyone is on a mission first thing in the morning. We get the kids to school on time. We *actually* get to work with a few minutes to spare. Everything seems to be in forward motion.

Some days it feels like the whole world is sitting on our shoulders. The alarm didn't go off... or we slept through it. We find out a school project is due today and our child is having a meltdown... or we are! Everything that can go wrong, seems to do just that! What do you do? What CAN you do? Have you ever found yourself saying, "I just want to go back to bed and hide under the covers"?

Whether you are hanging tough, or barely hanging on... the ONE thing that can change our outlook on the day is turning our minds and our hearts toward God. Regardless of how much time you have to sit in His presence at the start of your day, take a moment to pause and breathe deeply, even if you have to multitask due to oversleeping.

Thank God for helping you to even function. Ask Him to help you focus and take today one step at a time. Even when things are hurried, flurried, and scurried… and especially when nothing before you seems to make sense, God is in control and He won't leave you to figure it all out by yourself.

Romans 8:28 (CEV) tells us, *We know that God is always at work for the good of everyone who loves Him. They are the ones God has chosen for His purpose.* Don't miss this thought… that God is *at work*. You set out to do what you can and watch for God to do what only He can do.

God is at work

Guilt-Free Timekeeping

I recently saw a brilliant billboard. The gigantic sign on the highway was completely white with a picture of a single Timex watch in the center... and one sentence, "Know the time without seeing you have 1,249 unanswered emails."

It's come to that, hasn't it? I haven't worn a watch on my arm for a number of years. I always have my cell phone in my hand or within reach and use it, like... clockwork, to keep track of the time. The problem is - it's *always* reminding me of all the other things that I need to do.

Maybe going "old school" and wearing a watch again could help me manage my time better. Maybe there IS a downside to having everything in one place! Like when was the last time you used your Bible app in church, to look at the scripture your Pastor was preaching on, only to be distracted by pop-up notifications of texts, direct messages, or news headlines? I noticed this Sunday when I used my actual study Bible in church rather than my Bible app. I was less distracted and I did more note-taking!

There is something to be said about keeping the main thing - the main thing. If we want to be more efficient, keeping distractions to a minimum, we may have to make a change or two in the applications we use and when we use them. Trust me. I enjoy the convenience of having things all in one place. In Ecclesiastes 3:1, *There is a time for everything, and a season for every activity under the heavens.*

For me, it is an exercise in discipline. And if I really want to be able to go for a while without the guilt of having 1,249 unanswered emails... I'll wear a watch!

Live In the Flow

In the region where I live, depending on how close you are to the Atlantic, we are at or just barely above sea level. So imagine how my mind was blown when I visited the Dead Sea on the border of Israel and Jordan some years ago and learned that it is the lowest point on the whole earth at almost 1,400 feet BELOW sea level. It's so much farther from the sun that you have much less chance of getting sunburned there. The water was exquisitely turquoise. And even if you never learned to float... you *will* float on the Dead Sea. Why? It's estimated to have 37 billion tons of salt in it giving it so much natural buoyancy that everyone floats on top. With such a high salt and mineral content, it has powerful, natural healing properties so people travel from all over the world to visit and take advantage of these minerals. It is the largest FREE spa in the world!

It's known as the Dead Sea because water flows into it from the Jordan but it has no path to flow out. So the water evaporates and leaves the salt and minerals behind. The Dead Sea has so many vital ingredients in it but because it has no outlet... no living thing can live in it. Think about that. So many good things go in and because it bottles it all up without letting any of it out, it has no life within.

What if we choose to consume all of these good things? All the gifts and talents that God has given us. All the favor of God that He has bestowed on us. But we don't share them with others. We don't look for ways to use our gifts and talents for the glory of God to serve others—*what a tragedy!* 1 Peter 4:10 (CEV) is clear: *Each of you has been blessed with one of God's many wonderful gifts to be used in the service of others. So use your gift well.*

Let's not hold on so tight to what God gives us. Let's be willing to *live in the flow* of what God is doing in us and through us to those around us!

Giving Up Your Seat

When my brothers and I were growing up, my parents taught us that it was honorable to give up our seat to an adult, someone older than us, and for my brothers to always offer their seat to a lady. They taught us that we should always hold the door for the person coming up behind us, even if we have to wait a minute for them to get to the door. And that a gentleman always picks up something that is dropped by a lady. I love that they instilled those kinds of good behaviors in us.

Sunday after church when we were meeting my parents for lunch at a local eatery we arrived first. Some people were waiting to be seated in the front area with only a few seats. I had the thought that if I could find a seat I'd sit there until my parents arrived so they would have a seat while we waited. As I looked over at these two couples that looked to be the age I am (in my head), they got up to give my husband and me a place to sit.

As I'm sitting there, thinking about saving this seat for Mom and Dad, it occurs to me that they had no idea that I'm reserving a space for my parents to sit. They were giving up their seats for us, their elders! It is the cycle of life, I suppose. The upside of that moment, looking back, was seeing that parents are still teaching kids to have good manners and in their 30s… and 40s… they're still living them out! And if that was you and you're reading this - thank you again!

Kindness, especially unexpected kindness, is classy, beautiful, and memorable. And it's part of what God says reveals His love to others. Because love IS kind.* And it is blind to our age. Kindness can be exchanged no matter how young or old, and when it happens, we see a little glimpse of our Father. I believe that when it happens, if we listen closely, we might hear the Father whisper, "More! More of that!"

---

*1 Corinthians 13:4-8

Surprise And Delight

I'm not sure which is more fun... to be the giver... or the recipient of a completely unexpected gift. When you have the opportunity to do something kind for someone whether it is a stranger or your best friend, it gives YOU a happy feeling. At the place where I work, The Bridge, our team looks for ways every day that we can do something kind and unexpected for those around us. We like to call it, "Surprise and Delight!"

Sometimes it's the little things that can make the biggest difference in our day. Like paying for the order of the driver behind you in the drive-through when you pay for your own. Dropping off a basket of goodies or offering to help run errands or clean up after dinner. Surprise and delight! Both the giver and receiver are delighted!

I know we would have a hard time surprising God because He already knows what we're up to. But I believe that every time we choose Him, when we choose to pray, when we choose to spend some time reading His Word, every time we turn our heart toward Him in our thoughts and conversations with others, God is delighted!

And think about how often something happens that we didn't expect that brightens our day. At times we may be expecting God to respond to our prayer in a specific way. Most often He moves in a way we never anticipated. Because He always knows what we need and just when we need it.

I love this promise from God in Isaiah 43:19 (VOICE):

> God said, "Watch closely: I am preparing something new; it's happening now, even as I speak, and you're about to see it. I am preparing a way through the desert; Waters will flow where there had been none."

That's how God works. Surprise and delight. He is our greatest example of how to surprise and delight others around us. You won't have to wait long to see His handiwork. I believe He's working on your behalf even now and that He's got something good on the way for you today!

Dream Home

Imagine that you are building a house. Money is no issue while we're imagining this new house design. You can dream and design your perfect dream home. You tell the engineer everything you'd like and he or she gets to work creating exactly what you asked for. You review it. It's approved and the builder begins to bring your dream to life.

If you've ever gone through the process of building a home you know things happen, something unexpected, either too much or not enough. Maybe you realize you left something out or you've seen what someone did and you got back to the builder to add that in. But changes have a cost, and sometimes the change you want now isn't possible with the work that has already been done. And already... your dream home isn't what you want. In real life, you may have had to give up some things you really wanted because they cost too much or it's not feasible for the location or the space.

Did you know the Bible calls us the temple of the Holy Spirit? God, the Master Architect and Builder, designed and built us to His specifications which He planned for us way before we were even born. He left nothing out when He made us. But, He knew, that in this life, in this world that we live in… God knew that modifications would need to be made along the way. He counted the cost. His one and only Son, Christ Jesus, paid the highest price, to bring the Father's plan to life. Real, forever life!

Ephesians 2:10 declares, *For we are God's handiwork, created in Christ Jesus to do good works, which God prepared in advance for us to do.*

God designed us and created us to do good things. His plan is perfect and today… we have work to do!

The Race

If you've ever watched a NASCAR race you know the bulk of the attention is on the driver. The driver has to have disciplined his or her body for the length and stress of the race. They must stay focused on the track and any cars in front of them and they must be in tune with their own car. The goal? Cross the finish line first, or as close to first as possible.

But it takes more than an experienced driver and a finely tuned race car to win a race. Every driver has a team, and each team member has a specific role to play to help that driver do the very best in order to win. The pit crew is ready to jump the wall and race to replace worn tires, refuel the engine, and make minor adjustments in split seconds to get the car and its driver back in the race. The spotter sits way up high, can see all the other cars around their teammate and can communicate directly with the driver to give direction, encouragement, and immediate warning when there is danger. The thrill of the crowd in the stands cheering for their favorite driver is exciting and energizing.

When the driver wins... the whole team celebrates! My favorite part of the win is watching the whole crew run to the driver and high-five and hug and throw their hands up high to celebrate the victory. And if you listen you'll hear the driver thank the crew and crew chief, the owner and so on. Because that winner knows... they did not get there on their own. It was a team effort!

You and I are in a race. While we may feel, at times, like we are on our own, in this race, the Apostle Paul told us in Hebrews 12:1 (CEV),

> *Such a large crowd of witnesses is all around us! So we must get rid of everything that slows us down, especially the sin that just won't let go. And we must be determined to run the race that is ahead of us.*

We are not alone! God gives us people to come alongside to cheer us on, to help us AND He puts us in the pit crew of others to do the same.

We also have a spotter! The Holy Spirit can see *everything* and He will communicate with us, giving us direction, encouragement, and warnings of danger. The goal of *our* race isn't to cross the finish *first*. Our goal is to finish the race *well*. So keep running the race. Let's keep cheering each other on. Let's listen closely to the voice of the One who gave His all so we could truly run this race well. And that's the win!

What Is Your Ministry?

We know our home church is a ministry. There are many non-profit organizations that serve in a ministry capacity, and you could probably name some people who are involved in the ministry that impact you or someone around you in one way or another.

Do YOU have a ministry? Ephesians 4:11-12 (CEV) tells us, *Christ chose some of us to be apostles, prophets, missionaries, pastors, and teachers, so His people would learn to serve and His body would grow strong.*

Perhaps you are serving in one of those capacities. But many of us feel like we don't fit into one of those five.

There are some talents and gifts that open the door for us to be part of a larger ministry, and God wants us to use those talents for His purposes. Musicians, writers, and speakers may all have ministries. But what if you don't feel like you fit into any of *those*?

Did you know that we are ALL called to ministry? The ministry of *presence*... the ministry of just being there. Think of the last time that you were really struggling and someone just sat with you. Not trying to fix anything or pile on advice. To just listen and wait. Could that really be a ministry? You better believe it!

To be truly present, not sitting in the same room watching TV or scrolling through our news feed on our phone, but patient, peaceful, and prayerful. Present. That is a powerful ministry that you and I can both walk in as God leads us. The ministry of presence.

Unfinished

When my daughter, Abby, was in the first grade my husband and I received a surprising comment from her teacher at our first parent-teacher conference. The teacher told us that she was having trouble with Abby in one very specific situation. Abby did not want to leave classwork unfinished. Whether it was lunch, gym, recess, or a trip to the library, it was a frustrating interruption to her focus to complete her assignments. No matter how much the teacher tried to assure her that she could finish when she returned... she was not a happy camper.

The other day she told me that one of her most frustrating things at work are days when interruptions are so frequent she is not able to finish her workload before she leaves for the day. Sound familiar? My girl finds satisfaction in finishing the work. All these years later she still has that same work ethic.

I was reminded recently of a Bible verse that tells us our *spiritual* work ethic should hold the same level of importance if not more.

But my life is worth nothing to me unless I use it for finishing the work assigned me by the Lord Jesus—the work of telling others the Good News about the wonderful grace of God.

Acts 20:24 NLT

God has specific Kingdom work for each of us to accomplish. The work of telling others the Good News that Jesus came to save us. The news that God's grace is for everyone who will receive it. We have an assignment today. Tell everyone who will listen about Jesus. Finish the work!

The Hard Word

One of the hardest words in the English language for me to say over the years might surprise you. It's just two letters. It might even be a word that you struggle to speak. The word... is "NO." You may have spoken it successfully at times. I finally learned that I could say, "No" to some things.

For years I said, "Yes" to almost everything I was asked to do. I'm not talking about the obvious things that we know we shouldn't do. Some things that I said yes to were important things that I really needed to say yes to, and some were things I probably should have taken a step back from to have time for the important things in my life. Some were things I just really didn't want to do or didn't have time to do, but I said, "Yes," so I didn't disappoint someone, and, in the meantime, I missed out on what I should have been doing.

Even a good thing is a bad thing when it replaces the *best* thing. Saying, "No" to the good can give us the ability to say, "Yes" to the great! And I'm not saying that we should say no just to avoid doing things. I am saying that I believe the secret to knowing when to say yes OR no is what Jesus told us:

"Are you tired? Worn out? Burned out on religion? Come to me. Get away with me and you'll recover your life. I'll show you how to take a real rest. Walk with me and work with me—watch how I do it. Learn the unforced rhythms of grace. I won't lay anything heavy or ill-fitting on you. Keep company with me and you'll learn to live freely and lightly."

Matthew 11:28-30 MSG

I definitely want to learn the unforced rhythms of grace. Walking and working with Jesus will teach us how to be in tune with Him to know when to say "Yes" and when to say "No."

The Scent of Stress

Is there something you do when you're *really* stressed? My girlfriends always knew when I was feeling stressed because I would come in wearing brand-new perfume. I don't know when it started but I found myself shopping for a new fragrance any time I felt as if I were in over my head! After a dozen or so fragrances lined up on my dresser, I realized I had a problem and figured I'd better find a solution!

I discovered that when I called or visited one of my most trusted friends and shared my current situation or frustration she would listen intently, perhaps offer some advice, often remind me that it wouldn't always be this way, and always prayed with me before we said goodbye.

Proverbs 27:9 (NLT) sums it up so beautifully, *The heartfelt counsel of a friend is as sweet as perfume and incense.*

Little did I know that the answer to my specific situation was spelled out in God's Word! I love how God surprises us with nuggets of wisdom and directs our steps when we seek Him.

Whatever it is that you're stressing over today, God has the answer for you. He promised to give us wisdom in generous amounts when we ask Him for it. Ask Him today. Sit for a bit in His presence and listen for His response. He is waiting for you now!

Holding Patterns

My friend and I were flying to Cincinnati to be in a mutual friend's wedding and to celebrate the new chapter in her life. At that point in my life, I had only flown a handful of times, but even as inexperienced as I was, I could tell, after a while, that we were flying in a big loop. We knew we were scheduled to land in Cincinnati at a certain time, however, it was well past that time and we didn't seem to be making a descent to our destination.

Then the captain made an announcement that due to a very bad storm, we were in a holding pattern maintaining our position above the storm clouds, over the city that had lost a large portion of its electricity during this storm.

We were frustrated. Concerned that those who were waiting on us would be waiting much longer than expected to pick us up. Even some FOMO. You know… "Fear of Missing Out" of the festivities, that were probably starting without us!

That holding pattern was such an inconvenience! But, really, that holding pattern saved our lives! Keeping us above the storm was not at all what we wanted, but it was definitely what we needed. And how often do we find ourselves frustrated with our circumstances, feeling as though we are in a holding pattern, as though nothing seems to change? Maybe that holding pattern is keeping us above the clouds of disaster, some storm that is brewing just beyond our foresight, and God is keeping us safe from it. Maybe it's building character in us as we wait... or it's the timing of someone else's story that coincides with ours. Regardless of the reason, Romans 8:28 (CEV) reminds us, *We know that God is always at work for the good of everyone who loves Him. They are the ones God has chosen for His purpose.*

Whatever the holding pattern is that seems to be keeping you from what you've been praying for... God's timing is always right on time. And someday if God allows us to look back on our lives and fully see the intricacies of the details that God has orchestrated in our lives... we will have even more reason to give Him glory!

Oh God You are my God, early will I seek You

Early Bird Specials

What if God offered "early bird specials" to anyone who sat at the table with Him at the start of the day? What if we could go *into our day* with an extra portion of peace and joy? How about suiting up with the whole armor of God before we even get out of bed? Imagine having the time to sit and enjoy the meal without being rushed or distracted.

I drove by a restaurant the other day with a sign in front that advertised early bird specials. Essentially if you come in early you get a special price. There shouldn't be a problem finding a table, and if you prefer a quieter meal chances are good that you'll find that too. Thinking about the benefits to the early bird as I drove by that sign I started thinking about the benefits of coming to the Lord early in the day. How much better my days are when I turn my heart toward God first thing in the morning. Even when things go sideways in my day I find myself leaning into Jesus faster than any day I went through oblivious to His presence.

Psalm 63:1 (NKJV) confirms it, *Oh God You are my God, early will I seek You.*

It's not just about seeking God early in our day but also early in every venture, every assignment, and every challenge. Seek Him early. The early bird special will be worth telling others about!

Lingering Longer

When I first began investigating the art of Bible Journaling I invited some of my friends to come with me on the journey and learn together. We each bought Bibles with very wide margins for drawing, creating, and making notes of what particular passages of Scripture meant to us. While I am not much of an artist I DO love to create. Colors and cloths. Paints and pencils. So many ways to tell the story of my thoughts and emotions about how the Bible is impacting and leaving a mark on my life.

What I realized quickly was that there was an art that I could aspire to... the art of lingering longer in the Word of God. As I sat with my Bible open thinking about how I would respond to His Word on the page I realized the value of lingering over - meditating - on His Words to me.

God tells us the benefits of lingering there in Joshua 1:8:

> *Keep this Book of the Law always on your lips; meditate on it day and night, so that you may be careful to do everything written in it. Then you will be prosperous and successful.*

And in Psalm 1:2-3:

> *But whose delight is in the law of the Lord, and who meditates on His law day and night. That person is like a tree planted by streams of water, which yields its fruit in season and whose leaf does not wither—whatever they do prospers.*

Whether we draw or make notes in our Bible isn't the point. If we really want to know God's heart for us and how we should live our lives - it all begins with this… lingering longer in God's Word.

Clear Plastic Covers

I was watching a movie the other night, that started with a friend sitting down on her friend's sofa that was covered in clear plastic. As she lifted a fork full of cherry pie to her mouth she asked her friend, "When are you going to take this plastic off and live a little?" You know what happened next, don't you? You guessed it! The cherry pie dropped right off the fork, onto the plastic and the response was, "That would be why I haven't taken off the plastic!"

My grandmother had certain pieces of furniture she kept covered in this clear, thick plastic and mostly as kids we avoided sitting on them because while they were protected from stains, they were not at all comfortable to sit on. Watching that scene from the movie made me think about how we tend to live life. Is it possible we have covered ourselves with a nearly invisible wall that attempts to shield us from really living like we were meant to live? We want to avoid the stains of life, but that's what brings color into the fabric of our story… and builds character in our soul. It's how we learn and grow.

Jesus said in John 10:10 (ESV), *"The thief comes only to steal and kill and destroy. I came that they may have life and have it abundantly."*

Two very important things to know, really know, about these words of our Lord. There is a very real enemy who wants to harm us, and Jesus left heaven to make it clear to us, beyond all doubt, that HE came to be sure we would LIVE, *really* LIVE!

Maybe it's time to take the plastic off the furniture. Stop trying to make everything look perfect and living afraid that we'll mess up the fabric of our life! Let Jesus come and sit awhile and in His presence He will bring abundant, extraordinary life to us. Life is so much better without the plastic!

One Lost Sheep

Ever lose sight of your child... in a store, at the beach, or the park? Remember how you felt? Panicked, distraught, even fearful? Remember the split second your eyes landed on your child? Relief! Gratefulness! The urge to kiss and hug them and then give them a VERY firm talking-to about staying where you could see them! I know, I remember it well. I think the words I said began with this, "If you EVER run off again...!!"

Luke 15:4-7 tells us a similar story:

> "Suppose one of you has a hundred sheep and loses one of them. Doesn't he leave the ninety-nine in the open country and go after the lost sheep until he finds it? And when he finds it, he joyfully puts it on his shoulders and goes home. Then he calls his friends and neighbors together and says, 'Rejoice with me; I have found my lost sheep.' I tell you that in the same way there will be more rejoicing in heaven over one sinner who repents than over ninety-nine righteous persons who do not need to repent."

Notice it doesn't say Jesus chastised the sheep all the way home. He *joyfully* puts it on his shoulders. He threw a celebration that HIS missing sheep was found! Have YOU experienced that moment when the Shepherd's generous grace and forgiveness found you in your lost-ness? Being the recipient… the one who was lost and is now… *found!* The Shepherd, who is Jesus, and all of Heaven, celebrates when each one of us opens our hearts to Him, asks forgiveness of our sins, and allows Him to rescue us and bring us home. That IS the best celebration of all!

When Good Isn't Good Enough

That's such a good movie! That restaurant serves incredibly good food! If you want a *really* good cup of coffee you have to try this coffee shop! We use the word "good" to describe so many things. When we have children it becomes a directive we give them from a very young age - to behave well. "Be a good boy. Be a good girl."

Even God used that description... as He created every living thing. Genesis chapter 1 records *God saw that it was good*. When He created Adam and gave him directions about each of those living things, verse 31 wraps up chapter 1, *God saw all that he had made, and it was very good.*

Then sin entered the world and we have struggled to be good *enough* ever since. Think of the very best person you know or have known about. It could be your neighbor, your friend, your parent, or your pastor... *none* are good enough for God! To be restored to relationship with God requires a goodness that we cannot attain by ourselves. Even Billy Graham and Mother Theresa, as good as they were, and as much good as they did in this world for others, were not good enough to stand in the presence of Almighty God on their *own merit.*

No matter how good we try to live - sin, the very nature of sin that we are born into, leaves us in a state of, "not good enough." But there is such *good* news. The *Good News* of the Gospel is that God's Holy Son, Jesus, was born and grew up, perfect, and blameless and He gave His life, conquering sin and death as He rose again. It is because of HIS goodness that we can be good enough to have a relationship with God.

On our own, we could never be good enough. But we are not alone. When Jesus is our Savior there is no more striving to be good. 2 Corinthians 5:21 reveals, *God made him who had no sin to be sin for us, so that in him we might become the righteousness of God.*

And THAT, my friend, is more than good enough!

Parking in A7

Whenever I fly out of the airport I always park my car in Long Term Parking Lot A. A is for Abby. Once my beautiful daughter, Abby, was born I made it a habit to always use that lot because I knew I would never forget which lot I parked in! Because A is for Abby.

The last time I found a great parking spot right next to the covered bench marked A7. As I was standing at bus stop A7 I was thinking about how I would remember A7 and I thought about what the number seven means to God. He rested on the seventh day. And hey... my word for this year is REST! How sweet to have that moment of remembering the journey that I've been on this year to discover all that God wants me to learn about rest, and He brought me to a front-row parking spot at A7.

When the shuttle bus arrived to take me to the airport terminal, as soon as I boarded, the driver said, "A7. Remember you are parked at A7!" In all my years of traveling, I don't think I've ever encountered a driver quite like this one. He clearly loved his job, loved people, and wanted to help everyone start and end their trip by remembering where they parked their vehicle. I love that!

Imagine if everyone we meet today went out of their way to help us. What a day we would have! Now we know that we will most likely encounter people who are having a bad day. People who are struggling themselves and just don't have the energy to help someone else. But what if WE made it a point to help others today in whatever way we can? If we want to affect change in the world around us, it has to begin with US!

Colossians 3:23 (GNT) says, *Whatever you do, work at it with all your heart, as though you were working for the Lord and not for people.* THAT is the key!

change has to begin with us

Lessons from the Fishbowl

It all began when I agreed to fish sit for a co-worker while he was away on vacation. His little aquarium and goldfish came to my office and after a week— I was hooked! Pun intended. When my co-worker came back to work two weeks later he retrieved "Goldie" and I drove right to the pet store to buy my own tank... and fish... and all that goes with it. It wasn't long after that, we had a fish tank at home in our kitchen as well.

I learned some things through that experience. Some fish love company. They thrive when they can swim in schools of similar fish. And some fish, like beta fish, don't play well with others. In fact, they mostly have to spend time in their own little boring fishbowl because they puff up to scare off the others if they're in the same tank with other fish. I also learned that some fish will stay just about the same size as they get older and other fish will keep growing to the size of their environment.

Sound familiar? Come to think of it... we are a LOT like those fish. Some of us love to hang out with people just like us. We love the company. While some of us are just as happy to keep to ourselves and stick to the fringe. Sometimes, we just don't play well with others, and we find ourselves in our own little bubble, either of our own doing or because everyone else just doesn't quite know what to do with us.

I think ALL of us will grow to the size of our environment. We were made to fill the earth! God created the whole earth and all that is in it and then He made us. This is what happened next between God and Adam and Eve:

> *God gave them His blessing and said: Have a lot of children! Fill the earth with people and bring it under your control. Rule over the fish in the ocean, the birds in the sky, and every animal on the earth.*
> Genesis 1:28 CEV

I believe the fruitful part of that command wasn't just about having children. I believe that as God made us in His image, the Great Creator gave us creative gifts to do amazing things. Live well. Honor God and fill as much space as we can for His Kingdom and His Glory. Keep growing to the size of your current environment and watch for God to enlarge your territory.

Junk Drawers

I don't remember the last time I cleaned out the junk drawer in our kitchen. The owner's manual for my first Keurig (which has been replaced TWICE) is a strong indication that it has been a while! The stuff I found in there was unbelievable. Random stuff. Things I hadn't thought of or used in a very long time.

I didn't set out to have a junk drawer. It just happened. Something I held in my hand and decided not to throw away found its way into a drawer... and I just kept doing it. I've been maneuvering through several years of stuff to get to the Saran wrap and sandwich bags. Things I use nearly every day. Based on the amount of stuff I threw away when I cleaned it out the other day, I've been collecting junk for quite some time.

It's entirely possible that my heart has a junk drawer. Things I've experienced and have never quite gotten over. Conversations I've stored away that bother me when I have moments to think. Emotions that haven't been dealt with and sneak up when I least expect them. It's exhausting. Storing things up that God did not intend for us to keep shuffling through like an exploding junk drawer or sometimes more like a treacherous minefield.

What are we holding in our hand, or our heart, that God is saying to "Let it go"? Are we maneuvering through some things unnecessarily? Choosing to carry it instead of laying it at the foot of the cross and leaving it there? It's what we tend to do sometimes. And God is saying, let - it - go.

1 Peter 5:7 (AMP) is so clear:

> *Casting all your cares [all your anxieties, all your worries, and all your concerns, once and for all] on Him, for He cares about you [with deepest affection, and watches over you very carefully].*

There's no room for a junk drawer in His beautiful creation! Let Him have it!

Sticky Notes

Do you remember what it was like in middle school? It wasn't easy, was it? When my girl, Abigail, was going through that stage, I was already at work in the mornings when she would get ready for school. Other than stopping by her bedroom door to pray for her on my way out each morning, when she hit a really rough patch, I began writing a little note each morning and sticking it to her bathroom mirror. We didn't talk about the notes and I never saw them accumulate so I wasn't even sure they meant anything to her.

The other day, she was cleaning out her bedroom closet and brought a box out to show me her cards that she had collected over the years. Birthdays. Christmas. Easter. Then she pulled out a giant pile of wrinkled sticky notes and said, "Remember these?" Abby had kept all those messages in her keepsake box. Messages like, "I believe in you," "I love the amazing young lady you are becoming," and "I can't wait to hear about your favorite thing that happens today!" Just one or two little sentences per note, reminding her that I was *for her,* helped her get through the day. Yes, I shed a few tears when I realized that my words of hope *really mattered* to her.

When we read God's Word and take it to heart, write it down, apply it to our hearts and live it out, I can just imagine God having a moment like I did that day. Writing down God's heart for us in His Word was of such importance to Him that He breathed into it as He inspired men to capture it on paper. 2 Timothy 3:16 reminds us, *All scripture is God-breathed.* And in John 20:31, *These are written that you may believe that Jesus is the Messiah, the Son of God, and that by believing you may have life in His name.*

His notes to us are so precious… and the best place to keep His Words of encouragement… is hidden in our heart!

My Japanese Maple

Years ago, I made the comment to my husband, Ken, that I would love to have a Japanese Maple tree in our front yard. It just never happened while we lived there.

Seven years ago, we moved into the home we are living in now. It was January when we moved in and the tree in our front yard was bare so I didn't even think about what kind of tree it was. When Spring came along, I realized that the tree with no leaves months earlier now had beautifully rich, red leaves greeting me every day was... a Japanese Maple. I couldn't help but hear God's promise echo quietly in my heart, *Take delight in the LORD, and He will give you the desires of your heart* (Psalm 37:4).

Long before we knew we would live in this home God had prompted someone to plant a tree... specifically a Japanese Maple tree... that would be here when we arrived, to remind us that God knows the things we hold in our heart. He delights to make even the little things come to be.

My friend, what is that thing that you've been holding in your heart and praying over? Maybe it seems little on your scale and you think it's insignificant to God. Maybe it's so big that you're even a little afraid to believe that God would do it for you! Let me encourage you today to focus on the first part of Psalm 37:4. Take delight in the Lord. I love how *The Passion Translation* directs us in Psalm 37:4-5:

> *Find your delight and true pleasure in Yahweh, and He will give you what you desire the most. Give God the right to direct your life, and as you trust Him along the way, you'll find He pulled it off perfectly!*

Bonus Section:
A Place Set Just For You

Falling in Love

Have you ever wondered why people call it "falling" in love? Falling has never made me feel particularly good. I mean honestly...I think of pain and embarrassment when I think of falling! And yet, there is such a warm, joyous sentiment attached to "falling in love."

It's the getting-to-know-you stage. Hearts and flowers. Dinner and a movie. Discovering what makes the other happy and sad; and what their dreams and goals are for life. The more we discover the more we find ourselves talking *about* the person every time we can. When I first met my husband, Ken, I was attracted to his discipline, his navigational skills, and his lack of procrastination. If something needed to get done he got right to it! He's the only person I know who used a highlighter to track his travel on the Rand-McNally Atlas on our tour bus as we traveled all over the country. And even though our days were non-stop on the road, every day I watched him carve out 20-30 minutes to read his Bible and pray. I still love those things about him...although the atlas has been retired for GPS... I don't mind that at all. I don't think Ken does either.

Remember when we first "fell in love" with Jesus? We couldn't get enough of Him and everything felt different. We told everyone we knew about Him and how He made us feel! I love the story of Jesus with the Samaritan woman at the well. After that encounter, she left her water jar (like she completely forgot that she had gone there to—get—WATER!) and invited EVERYONE to come and meet Him too. The rest of them asked Jesus to stay a couple more days and so He did. Here's what John 4:42 (ESV) tells us:

> They said to the woman, "It is no longer because of what you said that we believe, for we have heard for ourselves, and we know that this is indeed the Savior of the world."

The experience of falling in love changes us. We begin to see everything through the lens of feeling loved. And with Jesus it is the beautiful beginning of a lifetime of learning to love like Him. Just like the woman at the well, I would encourage you to come and see the Man who knew everything about me…and even then He loved me…and changed my life forever! I am forever grateful that I fell in love with Jesus!

Practice Makes Perfect

I started taking piano lessons when I was five years old. I loved playing the piano so it wasn't difficult to get me to practice. In fact, some days I *needed* to play. My mom told me that she could always tell what kind of day I'd had at school by the way I began playing when I got home. My mood definitely came out through my fingers on the piano. It was as if I was working out my tension and frustration through the music. She could tell when I was finally able to let it go by the transition in my touch on the piano keys from aggression to enjoyment.

Do you remember being told "practice makes perfect" when you were growing up? It took me a while to learn that it's not really about perfection. None of us are perfect. That is something to celebrate! Because God made each of us different. We bring individuality to the gift, the skill, the presentation. You and I have lived different stories and those differences impact how we relate to each new day. When we add our uniqueness to our practice, we can make an impact in our world that ONLY we can bring. That's why it's so important to encourage each other that the world needs what we have to share!

There IS one constant in our lives, regardless of who we are, where and how we were raised, and what we've experienced… the one constant… is Jesus! He *is* the Word. He *is* perfection! So when we spend time meditating and studying God's Word we are filling our hearts and minds with the ONE perfect answer to every situation, conversation, and presentation.

Joshua 1:7-9 declares:

> *Be strong and very courageous. Be careful to obey all the law My servant Moses gave you; do not turn from it to the right or to the left, that you may be successful wherever you go. Keep this Book of the Law always on your lips; meditate on it day and night, so that you may be careful to do everything written in it. Then you will be prosperous and successful. Have I not commanded you? Be strong and courageous. Do not be afraid; do not be discouraged, for the Lord your God will be with you wherever you go.*

Practicing God's Word until it becomes our response, like breathing…now that is the worthiest and most beneficial practice of all!

A Mile in Your Shoes

When my husband, Ken, and I first settled down after three full years of traveling on the road in full-time ministry we soon found ourselves in unfamiliar territory: our own home. We'd had a home... if you could call a tour bus, complete with a handful of other young, crazy people who loved Jesus and music *always* with us, a home! I am not complaining. We loved it and planned to return to it... soon. One thing led to another, before long we had jobs, rented and moved into a house, and found ourselves... in a new season.

We had already been together for three years and for the first time, coming home meant just the two of us. Suddenly, we had a different dynamic to our surroundings, and it took some getting used to. Someone gave me advice that seemed a little strange at first but has become a cherished memory from those early days. The advice was this: when you are in prayer for your spouse - stand in his shoes. The first time just felt awkward. However, the awkwardness gave way to insight, understanding, and connection.

I began to ask God in my prayer time to help me see the world through his eyes, to understand what he was thinking and feeling. Standing in his shoes and praying for him allowed me to lean into how God saw Ken. I considered Ken's story and how different things had impacted him over the years, and *that* impacted my heart for him tremendously.

You know the old phrase never judge a man until you've walked a mile in his shoes. Aside from the directive that the Bible tells us in Matthew 7:1-2 (NKJV):

> Judge not, that you be not judged. For with what judgment you judge, you will be judged; and with the measure you use, it will be measured back to you.

We still fight the temptation to judge others every day. What if we could stand in their shoes? What if instead of *walking* a mile in their shoes, we could *stand* in them... and pray for them? And ask God to help us see part of their story, and help us to have His eyes of compassion for them.

Could I walk a mile in *your* shoes today? Would you walk a mile in mine? Standing in prayer for each other is a beautiful gift that God gives us to help connect us in this journey. It helps us judge less and love more. That's the measure that I want God to use with me. I hope you do too!

I Could Never Handle That

Perhaps one of the hardest parts of living is not as much the dying part, but the living with the loss part. It might be the death of a family member, an unborn child, or a dear friend. It could also be letting go of our dreams and plans that we've held onto for a very long time. Either way, living with the hole in our heart that remains once we've let go is devastating.

Sometimes the *fear* of loss is just as debilitating. We witness or hear of someone else's loss and we allow the seed of fear that "I could never handle that," take root in our mind. I heard someone say once that the definition of worry is "borrowing problems that might not necessarily be ours." How true that is! And most often, God has *not asked* us to handle that!

So many times I hear 1 Corinthians 10:13 misquoted or misunderstood. God never promised that He wouldn't give us more than we could bear. He DID promise that He would help us to bear it and get through it.

Any temptation you face will be nothing new. But God is faithful, and He will not let you be tempted beyond what you can handle. But He always provides a way of escape so that you will be able to endure and keep moving forward.
 1 Corinthians 10:13 VOICE

Here it is in its simplest form: don't fear what might come your way in the future, be confident in the fact that anything, ANY THING, that God asks you to walk through, HE will give you a way to endure it, and keep moving forward! So, the next time you are tempted to say, "I could never handle that," don't give in to fear. Be reminded that it is very possible that God is NOT asking you to handle that right now. Find comfort in His promise that if He does, *He will be with you* through all of it!

Traditions

Traditions are the stories that families write together. We learn them from our parents and grandparents, and we teach them to our children and grandchildren. One mama taught her daughter to prepare a beautiful glazed, baked ham, and one of the steps before putting it in the oven was to cut off the butt, or end, of the ham. The daughter grew up following the tradition until one day she wondered what would happen if she *didn't* cut off the end of the ham. In fact, she discovered that the tastiest, most juicy part of the ham WAS the part she was cutting off! So, she called her mom and asked why she always cut off the end. Her mom responded that HER mom had always done it that way. Then, the daughter called her grandmother and asked, "Grandma, why do you always cut off the butt of the ham?" Her grandma answered, "Because my oven is small, and I have a small tray. The ham just doesn't fit!"

I wonder how many traditions we've held onto because they've been passed down through our families, and we don't even know how they got started?! When my husband, Ken, and I first got married and brought our family's traditions together, we had the opportunity to determine which traditions we would keep and teach to our kids and which of them we would not. I confess that today I am wondering about some of the things I do like my mother did, and do I really know the reasons why?

The best traditions we can pass along to our children and anyone else we have the opportunity to influence is our faith and our worship and adoration of our Father God. While the reason we believe, follow, and worship God is deeply personal, how it all began is historically documented, preserved, and clearly defined, in God's Word.

When it comes to our faith in God, we cannot rely solely on what our parents taught us or what we learned in Sunday School growing up. Our faith is meant to be a personal discovery and journey with our Creator. Hebrews 11:6 reveals to us:

> *Without faith it is impossible to please God, because anyone who comes to Him must believe that He exists and that He rewards those who earnestly seek Him.*

That's personal! It is experiential because belief in God is more than words on a page, or parental traditions handed down. It comes from having an encounter and ongoing relationship with the Living God. We know, with great confidence and gratitude, when it began and why we believe.

Repurposed

I had a dream that The Bridge, the radio station where I work, hosted a very large event. As we checked in all the attendees for this gathering, we handed them each a bag. I noticed the little tag on the inside seam read, "Made from recycled materials." In my dream, I stood there holding this bag and wondered... what kind of materials had been recycled to make this? What were they originally made to do or be? Imprinted on the outside of each bag were words of hope. It was an encouragement for the one carrying the bag, and for those who saw its words.

When I woke up from the dream, the first word that popped into my thoughts was... "repurposed." That bag was made of discarded materials that were broken down and carefully reformed or recreated to serve a new purpose.

That bag we were handing out to everyone…is a pretty close description of you and me. Before we come to know Christ as our Savior, we are headed in one direction, trying to find our way, living the best we can without knowing our real purpose in this world. Often what brings us to Jesus is realizing our brokenness, and our deep need to find purpose in our life. Once we meet Christ, He makes us NEW, and gives us a *new* purpose! 2 Corinthians 5:17 declares *Therefore, if anyone is in Christ, the new creation has come: The old has gone, the new is here!*

So much better than recycled or repurposed. We've been made new through Christ. We have a new purpose. I can't wait to see what God has for us today!

*after the
fire there
was the
sound of
a gentle
whisper*

Truth Is Quiet

Have you seen the movie "Jesus Revolution" yet? Based on the true story of evangelist, Pastor Greg Laurie, this movie tells a love story in more than one way. If you have seen it, then you probably know what I mean. If you haven't seen it yet, then I'll leave it for you to discover for yourself. Regardless of whether you lived through that era or not, it is a part of history worth remembering, and this movie tells the story well.

There is a scene in the movie where the Pastor is expressing concern to his wife about the conflict he's facing with his church. His wife leans in and says, "Truth is quiet. It's the lies that are loud."

It was a simple, quiet moment in the movie, but her statement resonated in my spirit like a 100-decibel loudspeaker! How often does the enemy bombard us with lies about who we are and about what God says about us? And the more chaos we find ourselves in…the harder it seems it is for us to hear the truth.

THE Truth...God's Truth...is most often a whisper. And when we determine to get quiet in His Presence...THAT is when we will hear Him. It is likely not an audible voice. But something happens when we posture our heart to hear Him speak that often results in clearly hearing His quiet voice above the chaos and the distractions and lies of the enemy.

If you haven't read 1 Kings 18 and 19 lately, I encourage you to read of Elijah's great victories as well as his battle with fear in those two chapters. How often have we had success in something only to find ourselves running off in fear of a threat? It happened to Elijah too. He found himself hiding out in a cave, fearing for his life. And after the LORD asked him, "What are you doing here, Elijah?" This is what the LORD said in 1 Kings 19:11-12 (NLT):

> *"Go out and stand before Me on the mountain,"* *...and as Elijah stood there, the LORD passed by, and a mighty windstorm hit the mountain. It was such a terrible blast that the rocks were torn loose, but the LORD was not in the wind. After the wind there was an earthquake, but the LORD was not in the earthquake. And after the earthquake, there was a fire, but the LORD was not in the fire. And after the fire there was the sound of a gentle whisper."*

The *King James Version* says, *...after the fire a still small voice.*

After all the noise and chaos of a windstorm, an earthquake, and a fire, Elijah knew the still, gentle whisper of His Maker. He waited and in the waiting, he heard the Lord. We will too when we wait. Past the chaos, the noise, and the lies of the enemy, we will hear God speaking to us...when we *patiently* wait *and* listen.

John 10:27 (NLT) Jesus said, *"My sheep listen to my voice; I know them, and they follow Me."* When we keep getting our hearts into the posture of listening, Jesus promises that we will hear Him!

About Denise

Denise T. Harper is the Program Director for The Bridge and has been half of *The Morning Show with Bill and Denise* from 2010 through 2023. Prior to The Bridge, she and Bill Sammons Jr. co-hosted *The Morning Show* on The Light FM for a number of years between 1991 and 2003. She is now co-host of *The Bridge Morning Show with Denise and Chris* every weekday morning.

After graduating from high school, she moved to Charlotte, North Carolina, to sing for a year at the PTL Club in 1982-1983. While there, she had the opportunity to work with many amazing artists including BeBe & CeCe Winans, Howard McCrary, and more. She left PTL to tour across the U.S. with The Spurrlows for a year. That experience led her to tour nationwide with the group, Sound of Joy, based out of Pensacola, Florida. It was in this group that she met and married her husband, Ken, who was already in the group and serving as the drummer, bus driver, and road manager.

Denise and Ken came back to Denise's home state of Delaware in 1990, not intending to stay long when God opened the door for her to work with the new (and first!) Christian radio station in Delaware, that was just going on the air. Her radio career started in 1991, and she hasn't "worked" a day since because she absolutely loves what she does. They are the parents of two awesome young people, Cody and Abby; and proud grandparents, "Popi and LaLa," to Cody's daughter Macey.

Connect with Denise T. Harper:
Email: deniseharpermedia@gmail.com
Facebook: facebook.com/motivesgirl1
Instagram: @motivesgirl1